Encyclopedia of Transportation

Volume 6

Macmillan Reference USA/An Imprint of The Gale Group
New York

Developed for Macmillan Library Reference USA by Visual Education Corporation, Princeton, NJ.

For Macmillan

Publisher: Elly Dickason

Senior Editor: Hélène G. Potter

Cover Design: Judy Kahn

For Visual Education

Project Director: Darryl Kestler

Writers: John Haley, Charles Roebuck, Rebecca Stefoff, Bruce Wetterau

Editors: Cindy George, Doriann Markey, Charles Roebuck

Associate Editor: Eleanor Hero

Copyediting Manager: Maureen Pancza

Indexer: Sallie Steele

Production Supervisor: Anita Crandall

Design: Maxson Crandall

Electronic Preparation: Cynthia C. Feldner, Fiona Torphy

Electronic Production: Rob Ehlers, Lisa Evans-Skopas, Isabelle Ulsh

PRINTED IN THE UNITED STATES OF AMERICA
1 2 3 4 5 6 7 8 9 10

Library of Congress Cataloging-in-Publication Data

Encyclopedia of transportation.
  p. cm.
  "Editorial board: Enoch J. Durbin . . . [et al.]"--v. 1, p. .
  Includes bibliographical references and index.
  Summary: An encyclopedia covering different methods of transportation and key events, people, and social, economic, and political issues in the history of transportation.
  ISBN 0-02-865361-0 (6 vol. set)
  1. Transportation Encyclopedias. [1. Transportation Encyclopedias.] I. Durbin, Enoch. II. Macmillan Reference USA.
HE141.E53   1999
388´.03--dc21
                                    99-33371
                                        CIP

Tanks

mobility *ability to move about*

Tanks are armored vehicles that move on continuous metal belts called tracks. Designed for **mobility** and equipped with heavy firepower, tanks have become the most important ground weapons in modern warfare.

History. In the 1300s, Italians built armored battle carts that were fully protected on the top as well as the sides. The first practical armored vehicles appeared in the 1900s. These early steam-powered tanks were light, carried machine guns, and ran on wheels.

By World War I the British and French had begun to build heavier tanks that moved on tracks and carried more powerful weapons. Tanks played a relatively minor role in the war until 1917, when more than 400 British tanks broke through German battle lines during the Battle of Cambrai in northern France. This spectacular action, though not decisive, demonstrated the potential use of tanks in ground warfare.

After the war the armed forces of various nations began to develop larger, faster, and more effective armored vehicles. The tanks of World War I could reach speeds of only about 8 miles per hour (13 km per hour), but by 1928 tanks produced in the **Soviet Union** could travel more than 42 miles per hour (68 km per hour). The newer tanks carried much larger guns capable of destroying armored targets at great range. As a result, tank armor became much thicker to protect against increased firepower.

By World War II, Germany and the Soviet Union had the best tank forces, with thousands of fast, well-armed, and sturdy vehicles. The Germans also developed new tactics for tank warfare. Instead of using small numbers of light tanks to support infantry, they massed heavier tanks into powerful striking forces. Such tactics helped Germany dominate the early phases of the war, but lighter-weight tanks with greater mobility later helped the United States and its allies defeat the Germans.

Soviet Union *nation that existed from 1922 to 1991, made up of Russia and 14 other republics in eastern Europe and northern Asia*

Modern battle tanks, such as the Challenger 2 shown here, carry a variety of weapons and equipment.

Modern Tanks. Since World War II, a variety of tanks have been developed for different uses. Lightweight airborne tanks can be carried by aircraft and dropped by parachute or unloaded after landing. **Amphibious** tanks are designed to cross rivers or land on beaches, and tanks equipped with snorkel devices can actually submerge and travel along the bottom of shallow rivers. Some tanks are used for support rather than fighting. They are fitted with special devices for performing such tasks as laying bridges or bulldozing away obstacles.

Modern battle tanks carry a variety of weapons and equipment. In addition to the large guns mounted on rotating platforms called turrets, many have machine guns, antiaircraft guns, and missile launchers. Also included on most tanks are radar for detecting planes or land vehicles and lasers and other electronic devices for measuring the distance to targets and keeping guns trained on them, even while moving over uneven terrain. Some tanks have special armor made of new materials to help shield the vehicles against armor-piercing projectiles. *See also* TRUCKS.

amphibious able to move on land and through water

Tariffs

domestic relating to activities or products made within a country

levy to impose or collect a tax

A tariff, or duty, is a tax on goods that are transported from one nation to another. Governments use tariffs to raise revenue or to protect **domestic** industries.

Types and Purposes of Tariffs. Import duties, the most widely used tariffs, are fees **levied** by the government of the nation importing the goods. At one time these tariffs were an important source of income, accounting for about half of U.S. government revenue until the late 1800s.

The main purpose of modern import duties is to protect a country's industries from foreign competition by raising the price of imported goods. Import tariffs also allow domestic producers to charge a higher price for their own goods. Although import duties may boost a nation's industries, they also encourage inefficiency by protecting businesses that could not otherwise compete with more efficient foreign producers. Tariffs sometimes lead to disputes between nations or to tariff wars. In 1999 the United States decided to impose duties on various goods from Europe in response to European tariffs on American bananas.

Export duties, taxes imposed on goods being sent out of a country, were once an important factor in international trade. They were largely abandoned in the mid-1800s, however, in an effort to encourage freer trade. A few nations still levy export duties. They do so primarily to discourage the export of agricultural or mineral products considered vital to the nation's economy or security.

Transit duties are tariffs levied on products that originate in one country, cross another country, and end up in a third. The nation through which the goods pass imposes the tariff. Transit duties once played a significant part in directing trade and determining the routes by which goods passed. But their main effect was to reduce the volume of international trade and to increase the cost of the products imported. In 1921 many of the world's nations signed an international agreement that abolished the use of transit duties.

International Trade Agreements. To encourage international trade, most countries have entered into agreements that either reduce tariffs or require nations to charge the same tariff rates to all their trading partners. The most important such agreement is the General Agreement on Tariffs and Trade, or GATT.

Established in 1947, GATT played a central role in promoting and expanding free trade around the world. One of its basic principles was most-favored nation status, in which countries agree to charge the same tariff rates to all nations that sign the agreement. Another important principle of GATT was that participating nations should provide equal access to their markets. In 1995 GATT was replaced by the World Trade Organization (WTO), a much stronger global organization created to oversee and regulate international trade.

Many nations participate in regional organizations or agreements that reduce tariffs and stimulate trade. Among the most important of these are the European Union (EU); the Latin American Integration Association (LAIA); and the North American Free Trade Agreement (NAFTA), which includes the United States, Canada, and Mexico. *See also* TRADE AND COMMERCE.

Taxis

A taxi, or taxicab, is a vehicle that can be hired to take passengers from one place to another. Most taxis operate in cities or suburbs. The term *taxicab* comes from a combination of two words, *taximeter* and *cabriolet*. Invented in 1891 by Wilhelm Bruhn, the taximeter was a device that kept count of the distance a vehicle traveled or the time passed while driving. A cabriolet, a carriage pulled by a single horse, could be hired to carry passengers.

The earliest taxi service was started well before the invention of the automobile. In the 1640s French coachman Nicolas Sauvage ran a fleet of 20 passenger coaches in Paris. The horse-drawn taxi continued to be used until the late 1890s, when electric cars made an appearance as taxis such as the Morris and Salom Electrobat. Shortly thereafter, automaker Louis Renault began producing taxis powered by gasoline engines. Major manufacturers of taxicabs since the 1920s have included the Yellow Cab Manufacturing Company, Checker Cab Manufacturing Corporation, Dodge, and DeSoto.

Most modern taxis are four-door automobiles that have been modified to stand up to the demands of heavy driving. Special features include stronger frames, springs, and shock absorbers than on ordinary vehicles. In Great Britain and some other places, an automobile must meet specific standards to be licensed as a taxi.

The fare charged for a taxi ride, often displayed on a meter located in the taxi, is usually based on the distance traveled and the amount of time the journey takes. However, some taxis charge a flat fee for a ride, and others use a zone system in which passengers pay a certain amount for each zone through which the taxi travels.

Companies that offer taxi service are organized in several ways. Some own a fleet of taxis and hire regular employees to drive them for a fixed wage. Others lease taxis to independent drivers. The drivers keep any money made beyond the cost of renting the taxi. Many taxis are run by owner-operators who purchase and drive their own vehicles. To operate a taxi, a driver must have a state taxi license. In New York City, a taxi driver must also purchase a special permit called a medallion, which can be quite expensive. *See also* AUTOMOBILES, TYPES OF; CAREERS IN TRANSPORTATION; URBAN TRANSPORTATION.

Telegraph

see Communication Systems.

Telescopes

radiation energy given off in waves or particles

The 200-inch (5-m) telescope at the Palomar Observatory in California was the largest telescope in the world until 1970. Updated with high-speed computers and electronic light sensors, it continues to supply astronomers with useful information.

Telescopes, devices designed to detect and observe distant objects, play an important role in space travel by providing essential information about the universe. Telescopes operate by gathering certain types of **radiation** given off by objects and using the radiation to create an image.

Italian astronomer Galileo Galilei became the first person to use a telescope for astronomical observation in 1609, when he turned a spyglass

toward the nighttime sky. Although small, the instrument allowed Galileo to see craters and mountains on the Moon, the larger moons of Jupiter, and many unknown stars. Later inventors developed various kinds of more powerful telescopes.

Optical telescopes collect and focus the radiation found in visible light. There are two main types of optical telescopes—refractors and reflectors. Refractors use glass lenses to bend light and center it on a single point. Reflectors bounce light off curved mirrors and direct it to a point. Many of the largest telescopes in the world are reflectors.

Other types of telescopes detect nonvisible forms of radiation such as radio waves, infrared waves, ultraviolet waves, X rays, and gamma rays. To avoid the distorting effects of Earth's atmosphere on certain kinds of radiation, telescopes are often installed on high peaks or even sent into orbit as satellites. The Hubble Space Telescope, launched by **NASA** in 1990, is a large reflecting telescope capable of detecting visible light as well as ultraviolet radiation. From its orbit about 380 miles (610 km) above the Earth's surface, the Hubble has been observing the planets and stars in our own and other galaxies.

NASA *National Aeronautics and Space Administration, the U.S. space agency*

Tereshkova, Valentina
Russian cosmonaut

Soviet Union *nation that existed from 1922 to 1991, made up of Russia and 14 other republics in eastern Europe and northern Asia*

In 1963 Valentina Tereshkova became the first woman to fly a spacecraft. Born in 1937 near Yaroslavl, Russia, Tereshkova worked in a textile factory and was an amateur parachutist. In 1961 after the **Soviet Union** launched *Vostok 1*, the first spacecraft to circle the Earth, she volunteered and was accepted in a training program for cosmonauts—the Soviet equivalent of astronauts.

On June 16, 1963, Tereshkova was selected to go into space as a pilot aboard *Vostok 6*. She orbited the Earth 48 times in less than 71 hours, before landing in Kazakhstan, Central Asia, on June 19. The Soviet Union named Tereshkova a hero and awarded her many prizes. *See also* Cosmonauts; Space Exploration.

Tires

A tire is a ring of metal or rubber around the outer rim of a wheel. Tires provide traction and grip the surface of the road. They also absorb shocks caused by movement over rough surfaces. Most modern tires are made of rubber filled with pressurized air. The air helps support the weight of a vehicle. Most vehicles that travel on land—automobiles, trucks, buses, motorcycles, bicycles, and even airplanes—as well as various types of machinery use tires.

History of Tires. For many years, carts, carriages, and other road vehicles were equipped with wooden wheels and steel tires. Though durable, steel tires did not provide enough traction and resulted in a bumpy ride. Various new types of tires appeared in the mid-1800s.

In 1845 English engineer Robert W. Thomson invented the **pneumatic** tire, which had an air-filled rubberized canvas inner tube with a leather covering. These tires did much less damage to roads than metal tires, and the air acted as a cushion and produced a more comfortable ride.

pneumatic *filled with or operated by compressed air*

On this tire assembly line in an automobile factory, tires are placed on rims.

However, the pneumatic tires lacked strength, and they did not become popular.

Instead, various vehicle makers started using solid rubber tires, introduced about the same time. These tires were durable, but they gave a rough ride because they absorbed the shock of bumps and transmitted it directly to the vehicle and its occupants. Solid rubber tires also damaged road surfaces, and in England laws were passed banning their use.

In 1888 Irish veterinarian John Dunlop "reinvented" the pneumatic tire. Inspired by his son, who complained about his bicycle's rough ride, Dunlop created a bicycle tire consisting of a canvas pocket with a rubber inner tube filled with compressed air. Covering the canvas pocket were rubber strips that thickened where the tire met the road surface. The Dunlop tire had great success, and later inventors developed pneumatic tires for automobiles and trucks. Most modern vehicles ride on pneumatic tires. However, some farm machinery and military vehicles use solid rubber tires, which are less likely to be cut up or punctured by rough surfaces.

Modern Tire Design. The 1950s saw the invention of tubeless pneumatic tires. In these tires, the rubber inner tube is replaced by layers of stiff rubberized cord fabric—each layer is called a ply—embedded in a rubber covering. The layers of ply and rubber covering form a hollow space that is filled with compressed air.

Tubeless tires are both more durable and safer than tires with inner tubes. When punctured, an inner tube can suffer a blowout, or explosion, which can cause a driver to lose control of the vehicle. If a tubeless tire is punctured, the layers of ply help slow down the rate at which air escapes, preventing a blowout.

There are three basic types of tubeless tires: bias-ply, bias-belted, and radial. In bias-ply tires, the layers of cord fabric are laid over one another at a bias, or angle, between opposite rims. Bias-belted tires are similar but also have several layers of cord fabric belts between the diagonal plies and the tread, or outer surface, of the tire. In radial tires the cord plies run straight across the tire instead of at an angle, and there are belts, usually made of steel wire mesh, between those plies and the tread.

The tread is an important part of every rubber tire. It contains a pattern of grooves and small slits cut into the surface that makes contact with the road. Tread patterns vary widely, creating surfaces that are suitable for various road conditions. The grooves in the tread channel away water, keeping more of the tire surface in contact with the road for better traction.

Modern tires are made of a variety of rubber compounds, corded fabrics, metal wires, and other materials. Different mixes of these materials are used, depending on the purpose of the tires and the types of vehicles for which they are designed. *See also* AUTOMOBILES, PARTS OF; AUTOMOBILES: RELATED INDUSTRIES; WHEELS.

Titanic

One of the most famous ships of all time became one of the most tragic shipwrecks on its maiden voyage in 1912. The sinking of the luxury liner *Titanic* has been the subject of many books, television documentaries, and movies, including a phenomenally popular 1997 film of the same name.

Part of the public's fascination with the *Titanic* stems from the fact that the ship's builders, Britain's White Star line, called it the safest vessel ever made and claimed that it was unsinkable. The *Titanic*'s hull consisted of 16 compartments, each watertight, and the ship was supposed to remain afloat even if as many as four of these compartments flooded.

Built by Holland Wolff in Belfast, Northern Ireland, the *Titanic* was the largest ship in the world, measuring 882.5 feet (269 m) in length and weighing 46,328 tons. It was also the most luxurious, with elegant staterooms and dining rooms for first-class passengers. On its first crossing the vessel carried some of the richest and most powerful people in the United States, including John Jacob Astor IV and Benjamin Guggenheim. Lower decks housed passengers traveling in less style, many of them immigrants bound for the United States.

The *Titanic* left Southampton, England, on April 10 with more than 2,200 people aboard, bound for New York City. Its route was through the North Atlantic waters near the island of Newfoundland. Although the captain had received warnings of icebergs in the region, he hurried through the night in the hope of setting a **transatlantic** speed record. On the night of April 14 the ship struck a berg. Five of the hull compartments opened, and water poured in.

The great ship sank in less than three hours. About 1,500 people perished either in the sinking vessel or while floating in the freezing water waiting for help. Far fewer lives might have been lost if the ship had carried enough lifeboats and if the passengers and crew had been properly instructed in how to use them. Other ships hearing *Titanic*'s distress

transatlantic *relating to crossing the Atlantic Ocean*

On April 10, 1912, the Titanic left Southampton, England, on its ill-fated maiden voyage across the Atlantic Ocean.

calls either ignored the urgent plea for help or were too far away to provide aid. After the disaster the International Convention for Safety at Sea drew up new rules requiring sufficient lifeboat space and lifeboat drills, and the International Ice Patrol began warning ships of iceberg danger.

In 1985 an American and French team of scientists located the wreck of the *Titanic* lying on the seabed at a depth of around 13,100 feet (3,993 m), and remote-controlled cameras broadcast images of the ghostly wreck to television audiences around the world. Investigators determined that instead of ripping a single huge gash in the hull, the collision had caused seams between the hull plates to crumple or loosen, allowing water to flood the compartments. *See also* SHIPWRECKS.

Tolls

A toll is a fee for using roads, bridges, canals, tunnels, and other **facilities** related to transportation. These fees help cover construction and maintenance costs of the facilities. Travelers have been paying tolls since ancient times—a toll road existed in India as early as 320 B.C. Tolls remain in use in many places today.

facilities something built or created to serve a particular function

History of Tolls. During the Middle Ages tolls paid for the construction and operation of many bridges in Europe. In some cases, as at the Old London Bridge, boats paid a fee to pass under the bridge. A local organization called a corporation, or perhaps a religious order or hospital, would control the bridge and collect the tolls. Foot travelers, horseback riders, and wagons were charged different amounts.

Usually a barrier across the road or bridge halted travelers until the toll was paid. Such a barrier might consist of a turnpike—a rotating bar with spears or pikes on it—or a tollgate, which could be opened once the fee was paid. Toll bridges and privately financed toll roads, known as turnpikes, were common in England after 1700. However, the public sometimes reacted violently to the idea of paying to use the roads.

In North America the first toll bridge began operation in Massachusetts in the 1650s. Toll roads appeared in the late 1700s, and many were in use by the 1830s. Around the same time, tolls played a major role in financing the construction of canals. When canals and railroads took over most freight hauling, toll roads fell out of favor.

The arrival of the automobile led to a burst of road building. Tolls paid for many of the new roads, including the Pennsylvania Turnpike in the 1930s. In exchange for tolls, the motorist had access to a well-surfaced road along which traffic moved smoothly because cars could enter only at certain points. Toll-road construction boomed again in the late 1940s, but the federal Interstate Highway System created in 1956 added many freeways to the nation's road system.

Tolls Today. Highway and bridge construction projects are expensive. Private investors may fund such projects with tolls under an arrangement called build-operate-transfer. The system allows the organization that builds the facility to collect tolls until it has been repaid for construction costs, after which the government becomes the owner.

In the past, travelers paid tolls in cash. By the 1980s some facilities issued seasonal or yearly passes to be displayed in the windows of frequent users' vehicles. The 1990s saw the introduction of new technology that

On the New Jersey Turnpike and many other expressways, drivers must stop at tollbooths to pay a fee for the use of the road.

simplified and sped up the process of paying tolls. The system allowed vehicles equipped with electronic devices called transponders on their windshields to drive slowly through toll collection points without stopping. Monitoring instruments recorded the passage of each vehicle with a transponder and sent the information to a processing center, which charged the amount of the toll to the traveler's account. The first completely electronic toll highway opened in Toronto, Canada, in 1997. The system operates without large staffs of toll collectors. It also reduces air pollution by moving traffic through toll plazas more quickly. *See also* Roads.

Tourism

Travel for pleasure—tourism—is a relatively recent development. But as millions of people throughout the world join the ranks of tourists, visiting attractions from beaches and battlefields to theme parks and sophisticated cities, tourism has become an important industry.

Modern tourism involves many types of travel. Some people enjoy basking in warm, sunny vacation spots in winter. Others want to shop, visit museums, or learn a language in a foreign country. The growth of tourism has opened up most of the world to visitors, transforming some poor regions into prosperous tourist destinations. But tourism has also created problems for local cultures and environments.

History of Tourism

The word *travel* comes from an old French word *travail,* meaning "work" or "hardship." The origin of the word reflects the difficulties that early travelers had to endure, such as dangers from wild animals or bandits, lack of accommodations, and the general hardships of moving around in early forms of transportation.

Wealthy Romans may have been the first true tourists, traveling to resort towns on the Mediterranean coast to escape the heat, dirt, and noise of the city of Rome. For more than 1,000 years after the fall of Rome, travel changed very little. Only the very rich could afford to travel safely and with some degree of comfort. The average person was too poor and too busy working to even dream about making a trip. Even among the wealthy, travel was limited by the difficulty of journeying long distances.

The situation began to change with the coming of the Industrial Revolution in the late 1700s and 1800s. The growth of industry brought greater prosperity and the appearance of a middle class with more money and leisure time. Railroads and steamships also made travel faster, cheaper, and more comfortable. Suddenly travel was not only possible for a good number of people, it was also a more enjoyable experience.

The appearance of automobiles in the early 1900s led to a dramatic change. Shorter work weeks and paid vacations became common in the mid-1900s, opening up tourism to more working-class people. The growth of airlines created a tremendous increase in international tourism beginning in the 1960s, and hundreds of millions of people now travel for pleasure each year.

These ten countries ranked as the most popular tourist destinations in the late 1990s.

Major Tourism Destinations	
Country	**Number of Arrivals (in Millions)**
France	66.8
United States	48.9
Spain	43.4
Italy	34.0
United Kingdom	26.0
China	23.7
Poland	19.5
Mexico	18.6
Canada	17.5
Czech Republic	17.4

Source: World Tourism Organization.

Tours and Destinations

Everyone has different ideas about the way to travel and the things to do on vacation. Some people look for independence and flexibility; others prefer to have trips planned in advance to avoid unpleasant surprises. Many people take vacations to relax; others seek out adventure, sports instruction, and even danger. There are various types of tours and destinations to suit the needs and desires of tourists.

Types of Tours. In 1845 British missionary Thomas Cook opened a travel agency, the world's first. Cook specialized in organizing escorted excursions throughout Europe. These were the first package tours.

In a package tour the tourist receives transportation, meals, lodging, and sightseeing for a fixed price. Package tours are popular for two reasons. First, they are often cheaper than other types of travel because tour operators can purchase large blocks of airplane seats and hotel rooms at a discount. Second, package tours take much of the uncertainty and hassle out of travel because everything—the travel schedule, hotel reservations, places to visit, and daily activities—is arranged in advance.

Some package tours have professional escorts who accompany travelers to make sure everything runs smoothly. Others arrange for hosts to be at destinations to answer questions and help travelers. Escorts and hosts also help take care of details such as handling baggage, changing money, and dealing with hotels and airlines.

pilgrimage journey to a sacred place

Although many people enjoy the security of package tours, others prefer to travel and make trip arrangements on their own. Independent travel offers freedom and flexibility. It allows individuals to go when and where they want and to plan their own activities. But going without a group generally costs more than package tours. Many tour operators offer packages that provide only basic elements of travel, such as airfare and lodging. Everything else is left up to the tourist.

Students have various opportunities for traveling. Study-abroad programs allow college students to spend time in a foreign country. Home stay or exchange programs offer high school and college students the opportunity to live abroad for a few weeks or months, often with a family. Many young people travel independently. In many cases, they can obtain special rates on transportation, accommodations, and entrance fees to museums and other attractions.

Types of Destinations. Beaches and mountain resorts have long been among the most popular tourist destinations. Natural wonders such as Niagara Falls, the Grand Canyon, and the geysers and wildlife of Yellowstone National Park are major tourist sites. Wilderness areas also attract visitors. A branch of the tourist industry known as ecotourism has emerged to serve the needs of those who want to spend time in natural areas without disturbing the environment.

Cultural attractions, including museums, music festivals, historic buildings, and religious sites, draw many visitors. Tourism of this kind dates back to the **pilgrimages** of the Middle Ages and the Grand Tour of the 1800s—a lengthy journey to the cultural centers of Europe by wealthy young aristocrats.

Special interests ranging from shopping and theater to antique collecting and bird-watching have become the focus of travel plans for many people. Vacations devoted to skiing, golf, scuba diving, biking, or other sports are very popular as well. Tourists also choose destinations because of nearby theme parks or seasonal events, such as the Bluegrass Festival in Missouri.

With the expansion of international air travel, many people can plan trips to exotic locations, such as the Amazon rain forest and the Himalayas, that once required a great deal of time and money to visit. Although tourism started as an activity for the wealthy, it has become an opportunity for a wide range of people to pursue various interests and activities.

The Effects of Tourism

Tourism has another side. It not only provides travelers with the chance to experience different cultures and environments, but it also affects the people and places visited.

Tourism can have a dramatic impact on the economies of destinations. Travelers spend money in the course of their visits. These funds may benefit the economy, providing income for local businesses and creating jobs. But tourism can also contribute to economic problems, particularly in developing countries. If poor countries borrow money to finance the development of tourist sites, they can build up large debts that must be repaid.

Tourism may destroy a local economy based on agriculture or fishing, replacing it with low-paying jobs in restaurants and hotels. Moreover, hotels and tourist attractions often use scarce resources, such as water and electric power, taking them away from the area's residents. Such matters can cause friction between the local population and the tourists, who represent forces bringing unwanted changes in their lives. Political unrest is another problem. The U.S. State Department issues travel advisories that warn tourists of areas that may be unsafe for foreign travel.

Concern about the impact of tourism on places of natural beauty emerged in the 1800s. Yet most tourists paid little attention to the effect their activities had on the environment. In recent years, however, the demand for more tourist development has led to increasing pollution of air and water at popular sites and to the destruction of landscapes. One of the most urgent issues in the future will be to preserve the natural beauty of tourist destinations as more and more people visit them. *See also* Cook, Thomas; Cruise Ships; Customs; Passengers; Passports and Visas; Travel Industry; Travel Writing.

Tractors

A tractor is a high-power, low-speed vehicle designed for off-road use in agriculture, construction, and road building. Most tractors run on tires, but some called crawler tractors are mounted on continuous steel tracks.

The earliest tractors, used during the late 1800s, were steam-powered plowing machines. Several people were needed to operate the tractors

Tractors represented an important advance in the field of agriculture. They allowed farmers to sow and plow their land much faster than old methods.

and keep them supplied with water and fuel. In 1892 an Iowa black-smith named John Froehlich built the first gasoline-engine farm vehicle.

In the next decades tractors became widespread. These early vehicles were used to pull tools such as plows. The power takeoff, invented in 1918, allowed tractors to drive other machines. During the 1930s some tractors were equipped with diesel engines that were more powerful and consumed less fuel than gasoline engines. Other developments include the use of **hydraulic** power to lift scrapers, scoops, or other devices attached to the tractor. Four-wheel drive tractors can handle jobs requiring higher-powered vehicles.

hydraulic operated by or using water or other liquids in motion

Tractors designed for agricultural work usually have two large, powerful wheels in the rear and smaller wheels for steering in the front. The rear wheels are spaced far apart, and the body is set high off the ground so that the tractor may be driven between rows of crops without damaging them. Most farm tractors weigh anywhere from 3,000 to 20,000 pounds (1,360 to 9,080 kg).

Crawler tractors are primarily used for construction, road building, and clearing land. Although crawlers are much slower than wheeled tractors, they can move extremely heavy loads and operate on steeply sloped surfaces because their tracks provide good traction. Crawlers also work well on soft or wet soil, where tires would sink. The largest crawlers weigh more than 70,000 pounds (31,780 kg).

Trade and Commerce

Throughout history, transportation and trade have been closely related. Trade—the exchange of goods and services—depends on the ability to travel freely to different places. Developments that make travel faster and easier contribute to a growth in trade. The transportation revolution of the past century has been accompanied by an unprecedented expansion in trade.

History of Trade

Trade arose long ago when groups of early people who had wandered from their native areas met and exchanged various items with other people. This type of simple exchange, called barter, remained the basis of trade for thousands of years. Commerce, the buying and selling of goods, came about only with the widespread use of money.

Ancient Trade. The Egyptians, Babylonians, Greeks, and other ancient peoples developed extensive systems of trade and commerce. Among the greatest traders of the ancient world were the Phoenicians. Master sailors, they established numerous trading centers throughout the Mediterranean region between 1200 and 300 B.C.

Early trade involved many risks, including storms at sea and piracy. As a result, most trade was limited to valuable items that could be carried easily, such as precious metals, exotic spices, and gems. Transporting bulk goods, such as grain or minerals, was difficult and much less profitable.

Much of the trade in the ancient Mediterranean world was conducted by sea, though overland routes also played a significant role. The famous Silk Road, connecting the ancient Near East with central Asia, India, and China, was used for more than 1,000 years.

The rise of the Roman Empire brought a great increase in the volume of trade in the Mediterranean region, as well as between the Mediterranean and Asia and other parts of Europe. Large Roman ships and the protection of Roman naval vessels allowed merchants to transport grains and other bulk cargoes more profitably and safely. The Romans' excellent and far-flung system of roads also contributed significantly to the expansion of trade during their time.

"Queen of the Adriatic"

The spread of Islam blocked trade between Europe and Asia after the 600s but did not end it completely. Much of the surviving East-West trade was dominated by Venice, a powerful Italian city-state on the Adriatic Sea. Strategically located between western Europe and the Arab world, Venice maintained strong commercial ties with the Byzantine Empire centered in Constantinople (present-day Istanbul). Its naval forces kept the eastern Mediterranean open for trade, and Venetian merchants served as brokers in the trade in luxury items between western Europe and the East.

tariff system of taxes on imported or exported goods

The Middle Ages. After the fall of Rome in the A.D. 400s, trade decreased dramatically throughout western Europe. However, it remained strong in the eastern Mediterranean as well as in Asia and the Near East. After the 600s the spread of Islam stimulated trade in those areas but, for the most part, cut off trade between Europe and Asia.

During the Middle Ages great fairs took place regularly in Europe, enabling merchants to meet and sell goods acquired in the course of their travels. These fairs flourished from the 1100s to the 1400s. During these years, trade in northern and eastern Europe was dominated by the Hanseatic League, a group of independent cities around the Baltic and North Seas. The commercial success of the league was due to its protection of commercial activities and promotion of free trade, which allowed the cities to trade with each other without having to pay **tariffs** on goods.

Several developments during the Middle Ages helped set the stage for the growth of trade after 1400. One was the Crusades, a series of expeditions by European Christians to recapture the Holy Land from the Muslims. Although unsuccessful militarily, the Crusades led to increased contacts between Europe and the East, which contributed to a revival of trade.

The Middle Ages also saw the development of new business practices, such as improved methods of bookkeeping, the use of standardized weights and measures, and the introduction of commercial banking and insurance. Such developments made trading both easier and safer.

Insurance became important as a way to protect sailing vessels and their cargoes. By reducing personal risk, insurance encouraged investment in shipping and other industries. Later, insurance was expanded to cover other forms of commercial transportation.

The Age of Exploration and Empire. Muslim conquests of the mid-1400s made trade between western Europe and the Middle East increasingly difficult. With many overland routes to Asia blocked by hostile Muslims, European nations began searching for sea routes to the Far East.

By the late 1400s European sailors had rounded the tip of Africa and discovered water routes to Asia. During the next century Europeans began to establish commercial empires in that region. The age of exploration also led to the discovery of the Americas, which opened a whole new hemisphere to European trade and settlement.

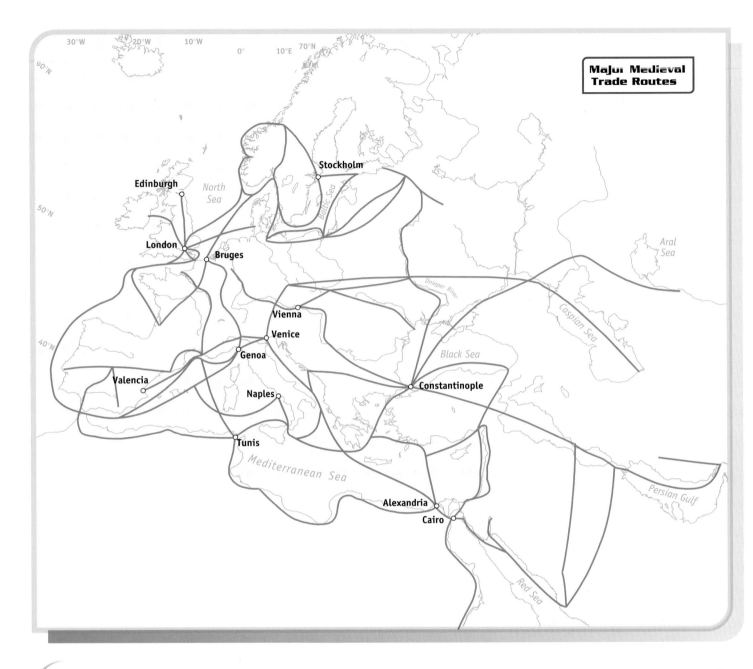

Major Medieval Trade Routes

During the Middle Ages, European trade flourished across the Mediterranean, Baltic, and North Seas.

Despite increased contact and trade with markets in the Far East, the establishment of European colonies in the Americas had a greater impact on international trade and commerce in the long run. Gold and silver from American colonies fueled the economies of Spain and Portugal and led to more widespread use of money in place of barter. New products discovered in the Americas—such as sugar, coffee, and tobacco—became major international trade goods. In addition, as the colonies grew, they provided expanding markets for European manufactured goods.

Trade with overseas colonies also led to the rise of new commercial organizations. To spread the costs and risks of trade, European merchants formed commercial trading companies. Combining the financial resources of many merchants or stockholders, the companies built their own ships and sent agents around the world to set up trading

monopoly *control of a market or product by a single company or country*

posts and colonies and to establish trade **monopolies.** Some trading companies governed colonial areas and even conducted wars for the parent country.

The breakup of European colonial empires in the late 1700s and 1800s signaled a new era in international trade and commerce. Up to that time, European nations controlled colonial trade through a system called mercantilism, in which all trade policies were aimed at producing wealth and power for the parent country. With the collapse of their empires, European nations could no longer dictate the terms under which trade would be conducted. Newly independent nations such as the United States focused on their own trading needs. They developed local markets, created separate trade relationships with other nations, and reduced their dependence on trade with Europe.

Modern Trade Developments

During the 1800s trade and commerce became transformed by a revolution in transportation. Larger and faster ships and the railroads dramatically increased both the volume and speed of trade. These developments were accompanied by a revolution in communications that helped link the world as never before.

Advances in Transportation. Until the mid-1800s, overseas trade was carried out by wooden sailing ships, and schedules were determined by wind and sea conditions. The development of steam power not only allowed ships to travel faster but also reduced their dependence on the weather. Ships could now operate on regular schedules, making trade more predictable and less risky.

As steam engines became more powerful, ships grew larger. By the mid-1900s diesel engines were replacing steam. Because diesel-powered ships did not have to carry tons of coal as fuel for steam engines, ships could carry greater amounts of cargo and travel faster and farther.

Meanwhile, inland trade expanded enormously in the 1800s with the rise of canals and then railroads. Travel and trade over land had been a terribly slow and difficult process. Trade routes might pass through rough terrain or areas with harsh climates. Wagon trains or caravans might be attacked by bandits or hostile native peoples. With canals, and especially the railroads, merchants could move larger loads at speeds that greatly reduced both the time and risks associated with inland travel. The canal systems of Europe allowed boats and barges to carry loads of freight at lower rates than the railroads. The completion of the Erie and Welland Canals in the 1820s opened shipping routes between the Great Lakes and major ports in the United States and Canada.

During the 1900s new forms of transportation—such as pipelines, automobiles, trucks, and airplanes—provided new and more flexible ways to move products to market. Towns not served by railroads were connected by highways, and goods could be delivered directly to businesses not located near rail lines. No longer tied strictly to the schedule of ships or railroads, trade could be conducted on a round-the-clock basis. In addition, airplanes made possible the rapid delivery of perishable cargoes,

Cargo ships carry agricultural products all over the world for distribution in local markets. Here, boxes of bananas are loaded on a ship in Costa Rica.

such as fruits and flowers, as well as overnight delivery of goods to almost anywhere in the world.

Advances in Communication. The late 1800s and 1900s also saw a revolution in communications that reduced many of the risks of trade. The telegraph, invented in the mid-1800s, connected the sellers, shippers, and buyers of goods, allowing them to share information on delivery schedules and prices. Later inventions, such as the radio and telephone, provided even more rapid ways to exchange information over ever-greater distances. More recently, communications via satellites, computers, and the Internet have tied together the entire globe. Today, even small merchants in remote places can make trade arrangements and track the movement of goods at any time from manufacture to delivery.

As the pace of technological change accelerates, barriers to trade and commerce between nations and peoples are rapidly being erased. It seems certain that continuing advances in transportation and communication will further increase the volume and speed of trade and commerce in the future. *See also* CANALS; CARAVANS; CARGO SHIPS; CHINA TRADE; CLIPPER SHIPS; COMMUNICATION SYSTEMS; CONTAINERIZATION; CRUSADES; FREIGHT; INSURANCE; MERCHANT MARINE; PIRACY; RAILROADS, HISTORY OF; SHIPPING INDUSTRY; SILK ROAD; SLAVE TRADE; SMUGGLING; TARIFFS; TRUCKING INDUSTRY.

Trade Winds

see Air Current and Wind.

Traffic, Vehicular

see Driving.

Trails

draft used for pulling loads

Before there were highways and superhighways, there were roads—and before there were roads, there were trails. A trail is simply a path, walkway, or route marked clearly enough for travelers to follow. For thousands of years people and their pack and **draft** animals walked along trails that wove together the web of human communities and led travelers, traders, invaders, and migrants from village to village or from one end of a continent to the other. Road builders laid the first pavements on top of ancient trails. Some modern highways follow routes that were once dirt tracks in the wilderness, pounded hard over time by the passage of humans and animals.

Origins of Trails. Wild animals seek the easiest routes while moving about in search of water, food, or shelter. As animals continue to follow the same path, they trample vegetation and flatten the soil. Scholars believe that by about 10,000 B.C. people were using animal paths, which became the first trails. In North America, Native Americans used buffalo tracks, sometimes called traces, as pathways. European explorers and settlers followed those routes. A Kentucky settler wrote in 1765, "We came to a large road which the buffaloes had beaten spacious enough for a wagon to go abreast."

People also created trails of their own to link important places, such as settlements, wells, and food sources. Though intended for local use, such paths often connected with others to form large-scale networks. Early European explorers in Africa, for example, claimed that they had crossed the continent on footpaths connecting villages.

As people followed some routes over hundreds or even thousands of years, they wore the surface deeply into the landscape. Walking on the path was like walking between two walls. In England some of these worn-in paths, called hollow ways or holloways, were more than 16 feet (5 m) deep. Settlers in North America commonly found Native American trails worn almost 1 foot (30 cm) deep, while a few hollow ways in New England were nearly 5 feet (1.5 m) below the surface.

Trails were not always straight. Often they curved to go around obstacles such as trees. In later years, if the tree disappeared, the trail would have a bend or kink for no obvious reason. The Chinese, on the other hand, sometimes built kinks into their routes to slow down evil spirits that might travel them.

Trails sometimes climbed to higher land, hilltops, and ridges to avoid marshy ground or flooding. Ridgeways, as such trails are called, date from 5000 B.C. in England. One of the best-known ridgeways in North America was the Natchez Trace, a trail originally created by buffalo on their way to salt licks near Nashville, Tennessee.

Important Routes. Trails developed hand in hand with trade and contact between people from distant lands. By 1500 B.C. tin from England, salt from Austria, **amber** from northern Europe, and other goods were moving along a network of European trails known today as the Amber Roads. More than simple paths for foot travelers and pack animals, these roads had beds of planks or logs in places. European trail tenders also laid piles of brushwood or woven mats to improve footing in wet areas and used similar materials to bridge streams that crossed

amber yellowish stonelike material used for jewelry

imperial relating to an emperor or empire

the trails. The Romans, ambitious road builders, later paved some of these routes.

In the Middle East a network of tracks spread outward from the **imperial** roads created by rulers of the Assyrian and Persian Empires between 1100 B.C. and 320 B.C. One of these tracks was a set of caravan routes that became a trade route between China and the Mediterranean after about 300 B.C. Known as the Silk Road, it contributed greatly to the exchange of goods, technology, and ideas between Europe and Asia. China began creating its own internal system of routes and trails as early as 1000 B.C.

European explorers and settlers in North America followed the pathways created over the centuries by animals and then by Native Americans. One of the best-known was the Iroquois-Mohawk Trail between the sites of Albany and Buffalo in New York. These tracks occupied such a central role in transportation that as late as 1808 U.S. government documents used the term *artificial roads* for routes that did not follow Native American trails.

New trails appeared during the settlement of the West. Chief among them were the Oregon Trail to the Pacific Northwest, the Mormon Trail to Utah, and the Santa Fe Trail to New Mexico. Thousands of settlers followed these routes across the continent, making them an undying part of Western history and legend. In the late 1800s the East Coast market for beef created cattle trails such as Chisholm and Goodnight-Loving. Cowboys drove enormous herds along these trails to cow towns with rail connections to the east.

Trails Today. In many parts of the world, local roads and major highways follow the routes of old trails. Some ancient tracks survive, however, and have been preserved as historic relics. For example, ruts carved by the wheels of heavily loaded wagons can still be seen along the remaining sections of the Oregon Trail in the western United States.

Another type of trail, the hiking trail, is a modern development. Built for recreational purposes, often within national parks and forests, such trails are open to walkers and sometimes to cyclists and horseback riders

During the 1800s traders in large wagon trains traveled along the Santa Fe Trail between Missouri and New Mexico. In 1848 to 1849, during the California Gold Rush, some 12,000 people used the trail on their way to California.

as well. One of the oldest and best-known hiking trails is the Appalachian National Scenic Trail between Maine and Georgia. The Pacific Crest Trail runs along the summit of western mountains. The Bruce Trail crosses the length of the Niagara Escarpment in Ontario, Canada. In many places hiking clubs and government agencies are buying old, unused railway tracks and converting them to trails for hikers and cyclists. The Alexander Mackenzie Trail, which links Montreal with a trail to British Columbia, is an example of a third type of trail—one developed to mark achievements of the past or to promote national unity. *See also* CARAVANS; CATTLE TRAILS; OREGON TRAIL; ROADS; SANTA FE TRAIL; SILK ROAD.

Trains

see Railroad Industry; Railroads, History of; Railway Trains, Parts of; names of individual trains.

Trams

see Light Rail Systems.

Trans-Alaska Pipeline

embargo government order prohibiting trade with another country

Built at great expense by private industry in the 1970s, the Trans-Alaska Pipeline was one of the largest engineering and construction projects ever undertaken. Covering 800 miles (1,287 km) from northern to southern Alaska, the pipeline was a remarkable achievement in the transport of fuel.

Why a Pipeline? Two factors led to the construction of an oil pipeline across Alaska. One was the discovery in 1968 of large oil reserves around Prudhoe Bay on Alaska's north coast. The other was a 1973 **embargo** by Arab nations on sales of oil to the United States. The embargo caused a fuel shortage that brought on high gasoline prices and long lines at service stations. Many Americans believed that the United States should develop more oil sources so that it would be less dependent on foreign supplies.

Located on the Arctic Ocean, Prudhoe Bay is choked with ice much of the year. After oil was found there, a group of oil companies proposed building a pipeline from the bay to the ice-free port of Valdez on the southern coast of Alaska. From Valdez, tankers could ship oil to refineries on the West Coast of the United States or other destinations.

Environmentalists argued that the construction project or possible leaks from the pipeline could damage the Alaskan wilderness. Their objections delayed construction and led to some modifications in the pipeline's design. In 1973 Congress allowed the project to begin.

An 800-Mile Tube. Building a pipeline as long as the Trans-Alaska would have been a massive task anywhere in the world. The fact that construction took place in one of the coldest and most remote regions on the planet, with winter temperatures as low as −70°F (−57°C), added special challenges. At the peak of construction, 20,000 people labored on the project.

Completed in 1977, the Trans-Alaska Pipeline crosses two mountain ranges and 34 major rivers and streams. About half of the structure is buried underground, surrounded by insulation. In areas where the flow of warm oil would damage permanently frozen soil, the pipeline travels above ground. The supports that hold it in place are specially designed to flex during an earthquake, reducing the danger of a pipeline rupture. Electronic instruments monitor the pipeline, notifying operators when there is a break in pressure and a section must be shut down. *See also* Pipelines.

Transcontinental Railroads

A transcontinental railroad is a rail line that crosses a continent. Railroads built across North America helped open the continent to travel, settlement, and trade and thus played a central role in the development of the United States and Canada.

In the mid-1800s various groups in the United States began making plans to expand the nation's railroads from the Mississippi River to the Pacific coast. In 1848 Senator Thomas Hart Benton of Missouri convinced the U.S. Congress to finance a survey of a westward rail line beginning in his home state. Meanwhile, other groups began surveying possible transcontinental routes. Although none of these surveys produced an acceptable solution, they did provide a great deal of new information about the West. The route finally chosen ran between Omaha, Nebraska, and Sacramento, California.

In 1862 Congress passed the first Pacific Railway Act, which authorized the construction of a transcontinental railroad by two railroad companies—the Central Pacific and Union Pacific. The act granted these companies property on which to lay tracks, as well as large pieces of land on both sides of the tracks. It also gave the companies loans to be repaid over a period of 30 years. A second Pacific Railway Act, passed in 1864, increased the size of the land grants.

The Central Pacific began laying track eastward from Sacramento in 1863. The Union Pacific did not begin building westward from Omaha until 1865 because of the Civil War. Both companies had to lay tracks across difficult and dangerous territory. The Central Pacific, which had to pass through the rugged Sierra Nevada, brought in thousands of Chinese laborers to work on the railroad. The Union Pacific had to deal with Indian attacks in the Great Plains and crossing the Rocky Mountains. Irish immigrants and Civil War veterans performed much of the work for this railroad.

The two companies laid more than 1,800 miles (2,900 km) of track and blasted nine tunnels through the mountains. Their new rail lines met at Promontory, Utah, on May 10, 1869. Ceremonial silver and golden spikes were driven into the tracks to celebrate the completion of the nation's first transcontinental railroad.

At first the new rail line had little traffic, just one eastbound and one westbound train each week. During the 1880s, however, increasing traffic led to the construction of four additional rail lines across the United States.

This photo shows the celebration held at Promontory, Utah, following the completion of the first transcontinental railroad in 1869.

Other countries also began building transcontinental railroads. The Canadian Pacific Railway, which ran from Montreal to Vancouver, opened in 1885. The Trans-Siberian Railroad, linking the Russian capital Moscow and Vladivostok on the Sea of Japan, was constructed between 1891 and 1916. *See also* CANADIAN PACIFIC RAILWAY; CAPE TO CAIRO RAILROAD; RAILROADS, HISTORY OF; TRANS-SIBERIAN RAILROAD.

Transportation, U.S. Department of

The U.S. Department of Transportation (DOT) is the agency of the federal government concerned with national transportation policies. Its areas of responsibility include improving safety, developing and enforcing transportation regulations, working out international agreements related to transportation, and providing support for urban and state transportation programs.

History of the Department. Many federal agencies and offices have been involved with transportation-related issues. In the 1890s the Bureau of Public Roads (BPR) was created to advise the government on road construction and maintenance. By the 1960s the BPR had a staff of almost 5,000 people, working in a complex network of agencies and offices that dealt with transportation policy and planning.

Over the years various groups had proposed creating a single department to handle all these responsibilities. In 1966 Congress approved the formation of the Department of Transportation. The BPR and more than 30 other agencies became part of the DOT. During the 1980s the department took over some duties of the Civil Aeronautics Board, and in 1996 the DOT assumed most of the responsibilities of the Interstate Commerce Commission.

Structure of the Department.

Headed by the secretary of transportation, the DOT consists of nine major divisions and employs more than 100,000 people.

The Federal Highway Administration provides funds for states to build highways and bridges and ensures the safety of interstate and international motor carriers. The National Highway Traffic Safety Administration establishes safety regulations for motor vehicles and makes efforts to reduce the number of highway accidents, injuries, and deaths in the United States. The Federal Railroad Administration is responsible for railroad safety, carries out research to improve and update rail systems, and helps finance the Amtrak passenger rail system. The Research and Special Programs Administration deals with the safety, handling, and transportation of hazardous materials. The Federal Transit Administration encourages and supports the development of urban transportation systems.

Among its many duties, the U.S. Coast Guard enforces **maritime** laws related to shipping and navigation, carries out search and rescue missions at sea, and conducts inspections of vessels. The Maritime Administration supports the U.S. Merchant Marine and operates the U.S. Merchant Marine Academy. The St. Lawrence Seaway Development Corporation operates the St. Lawrence Seaway in cooperation with the Canadian government. The Federal Aviation Administration (FAA) oversees air traffic control and air safety and certifies pilots, aircraft, and flight schools. *See also* AMTRAK; CIVIL AERONAUTICS BOARD; COAST GUARD; FAA (FEDERAL AVIATION ADMINISTRATION); GOVERNMENT AND TRANSPORTATION; HAZARDOUS MATERIALS, TRANSPORT OF; INTERSTATE COMMERCE COMMISSION; NATIONAL TRANSPORTATION SAFETY BOARD; REGULATION OF TRANSPORTATION; ST. LAWRENCE SEAWAY; TRANSPORTATION PLANNING; URBAN TRANSPORTATION.

maritime related to the sea or shipping

Transportation in the Twenty-First Century

The twentieth century saw a series of spectacular advances in the movement of people and goods. Railroads grew faster and more powerful. Crude motor vehicles developed into sleek and efficient cars, trucks, and buses. New types of ships emerged that travel above the water and below it. Finally, early experiments in flight led to planes that fly faster than the speed of sound and to spacecraft that can carry humans to the Moon.

It is impossible to know what lies ahead for transportation in the twenty-first century. However, a number of trends are already clear. Various efforts are under way to improve the efficiency of vehicles; increase their safety, comfort, and ease of operation; and decrease their impact on the environment. In any event, computers will certainly play an increasingly important role in all forms of transportation and in planning, traffic control, and the travel industry.

Motor Vehicles.

Among the most important changes likely to occur in the cars, trucks, and buses of the future are new sources of energy. The gasoline or diesel engine is still the preferred means of power for motor vehicles. However, declining fuel supplies and continuing efforts to protect the environment from harmful **emissions** point to the need for alternative power sources in the future. By the year 2000,

emissions substances discharged into the air

DaimlerChrysler executives show off the Necar 4, an automobile powered by fuel cells that convert hydrogen and oxygen into electrical energy.

component *element or part that makes up a whole*

alloy *substance composed of two or more metals or of a metal and nonmetal*

researchers had made major progress on several alternative methods of propelling vehicles.

Small numbers of electric-powered vehicles have been produced in Europe, Japan, and the United States. So far, such vehicles have had limited success because they are expensive and can run for only short distances before their batteries need recharging. However, engineers are working to develop more powerful and longer-lasting motor vehicle batteries.

Researchers are exploring other power sources as well. Some future cars may run on natural gas and blends of methanol and ethanol—liquid fuels that can be produced from plant materials. These fuels are highly efficient and less polluting than gasoline. Another approach being tested is the use of fuel cells, devices that convert the chemical energy of fuels such as hydrogen and oxygen into electrical energy. Steam engines, gas turbine engines, and solar-powered electric motors are other possible power sources for cars.

Vehicles of the future will feature new materials and new automated **components.** Their bodies might be made of lightweight materials such as fiberglass, special plastics, and **alloys.** Reducing the overall weight of vehicles will decrease the amount of fuel and power needed to drive them.

Cars and trucks may have computer-controlled automatic driving and navigation systems. Engineers are experimenting with automated

sensor *device that reacts to changes in light, heat, motion, and so on*

Chasing a Comet

The European Space Agency is preparing the first probe designed to land on a comet. The *Rosetta* spacecraft, scheduled to be launched in 2003, will circle the Earth and Mars, gaining speed from the planets' gravitational fields. In 2007 the probe will head toward the comet Wirtanen, a chunk of ice and dust that orbits the Sun every 5½ years. *Rosetta* will reach the comet in 2012 and orbit it to map the surface and choose a landing site. Then it will release a lander to conduct experiments on the frozen crust. The orbiter will continue to accompany the comet as it speeds toward the Sun at more than 28,000 miles per hour (45,000 km per hour).

suspension *system of springs and other parts that supports the body of a vehicle on the axles*

payload *object placed in space by a launch vehicle; any type of cargo carried aboard a spacecraft*

aerodynamic *relating to the motion of air and the effects of such motion on planes and other objects*

highway systems in which cars are guided by **sensors** and electronic devices installed onboard and in the road. Traffic monitoring technology may be combined with electronic toll collection to adjust tolls according to road use. Tolls might be increased during peak use hours to encourage drivers to travel at off-peak times or to choose alternate routes. In the trucking industry, automated vehicle inspection procedures will save time and money and increase safety. Computerized freight systems will be able to load, track, and deliver cargo with very little handling required.

Many new developments will focus on safety. Cars might contain computerized collision-avoidance systems to help prevent accidents. A sensing device that sounds an alarm when a vehicle veers from its lane would alert drowsing drivers. Radar-based devices would produce sounds and visual images to warn drivers about hazards on the road.

If an accident does occur, sensors in the vehicle will register the collision and a message calling for help will be sent automatically through the satellite communication system. Another option is a recorder, similar to the "black box" in an airplane, that will record details about the impact and the car's speed, seat belt, air bag, engine, brakes, and other systems at the time of an accident.

Ships and Boats. Ships and boats in the twenty-first century will probably be able to travel faster and operate more efficiently. The use of nuclear power to propel ships may become more common, allowing vessels to cruise for many months without refueling. Marine engineers are exploring ways to improve the efficiency of steam, diesel, and gas turbine engines in ships, as well as experimenting with fuel cells and the ocean's thermal energy as sources of power. New ship designs might also make boats stronger and safer.

Railroads. Advances in railroads will probably involve safety and speed. Trains and crossing gates may be equipped with sensors to prevent accidents by detecting oncoming trains. New strong, lightweight materials are being tested for railroad cars, as are new **suspension** designs that permit trains to run at very high speeds over ordinary tracks rather than on tracks specially designed for high-speed trains. Also in development are quiet trains that glide on a cushion of air instead of on wheels and high-speed "maglev" trains that are held up and powered by an electromagnetic field.

Aircraft. Changes in aviation will result in aircraft that can fly at higher speeds with greater fuel economy. One experimental craft, known as a roton vehicle, is designed to travel into space like a rocket, deliver a **payload** into low-Earth orbit, unfold a set of helicopter wings, and then land at some point on Earth. Planes may run on new fuels and power sources, including solar and nuclear power, and aircraft designers and engineers will continue to improve the **aerodynamic** design of aircraft.

Vertical takeoff and landing aircraft (VTOLs), which take off and land like helicopters but fly like conventional airplanes, provide a way to relieve airport traffic congestion. Because VTOLs do not need long runways, small airports will be able to accommodate even large planes.

NASA *National Aeronautics and Space Administration, the U.S. space agency*

NASA has been experimenting with solar-powered high-altitude aircraft that can remain airborne for days or even weeks at a time. One such vehicle, the *Centurion,* is a remote-controlled flying wing with no body or tail. The *Centurion*'s propellers generate enough power to allow it to soar at an altitude of 100,000 feet (30,480 m). Remote-controlled aircraft of this type might be used to monitor changes in the Earth's upper atmosphere or to track storm systems.

Spacecraft. The twenty-first century will also bring advances in space exploration. The completion of the International Space Station will provide a new, well-equipped home base in space for research and exploration. Space **probes** will journey farther into the distant reaches of our solar system and galaxy. At the same time, human space travel may increase, and the transportation of passengers and cargo to other planets may become a reality.

probe *uncrewed spacecraft sent out to explore and collect information in space*

Projects being planned by NASA include missions to measure particles and X rays in the Sun's atmosphere and to study one of Jupiter's moons. In addition to government-sponsored missions, private corporations are likely to launch commercial space ventures within our solar system.

New technology may help space exploration expand its horizons. Light sails—large, thin pieces of reflective material—may be able to carry payloads as far as Mars. The sails would be powered by a beam of light from a laser on Earth. Researchers are also investigating nuclear-powered propulsion systems that might produce enough force to hurl a spacecraft to nearby stars. *See also* Aircraft; Air-Cushion Vehicles; Automobiles, Parts of; Communication Systems; Electric Cars; Energy; Engines; Global Positioning System (GPS); Navigation; Pollution and Transportation; Public Transportation; Railway Trains, Parts of; Ships and Boats; Space Exploration; Transportation Planning.

Transportation Planning

Transportation planning plays a crucial role in developing and maintaining transportation systems and **facilities** such as highways, rail networks, airports, and harbors. Planning helps ensure that transportation systems not only benefit the economy but also meet the needs of individual travelers.

facilities *something built or created to serve a particular function*

aqueduct *artificial channel for carrying water*

Early Planning. Planning has played a role in transportation for thousands of years. The ancient Romans carefully mapped out the construction of thousands of miles of roads and **aqueducts** throughout their empire. In later centuries people laid out canals, roads, railroads, and streetcar lines to create convenient routes for trade and travel.

Until the late 1800s the companies that owned the railroads, streetcars, and other means of transportation planned their routes independently. In the United States wealthy railroad owners competed to expand their networks and construct new lines.

It was not until the 1900s that governments became involved in transportation planning. Officials realized that solving traffic problems and other transportation issues would require research, organization, and careful consideration of the effects of any decisions. In the United States

Further Information

To learn more about transportation planning, including developing different types of transportation systems and the role of government agencies in planning, see the related articles listed at the end of this entry.

early highway planners began by collecting information about the growing numbers of cars and trucks on the road. They used these data to improve the design and capacity of highways.

During the 1920s and 1930s the U.S. federal government and state highway departments conducted studies of traffic volume in many different areas. The goal was to find ways to improve the efficiency of highways and roads, such as by adopting uniform standards for road signs and traffic signals.

In the 1950s transportation planning in the United States began to focus on future needs rather than on just improving existing transportation networks and facilities. Many cities formed special commissions known as transit authorities—for example, the Bay Area Transit District in San Francisco and the New York City Transit Authority—to oversee the development of their transportation systems. The Civil Aeronautics Authority provided government funds for airport construction and expansion. Road planning moved to a new level with the Federal-Aid Highway Act of 1956, which launched the construction of the interstate highway system.

Modern Planning. The basic goal of transportation planning is to identify existing transportation problems and needs and to predict future ones. The issues may range from constructing a new airport to finding a way to make a busy suburban intersection safer. Planners try to devise workable and acceptable solutions to each problem. This process often involves various government agencies, private businesses, community organizations, and individuals.

Planners use computers to analyze data about transportation systems, such as the volume of passenger and freight traffic, times of peak use, and the condition of roads and other facilities. Computers also allow planners to predict future traffic growth and to create models for solutions that take into account the terrain, construction costs, and other factors.

Planners weigh a variety of issues related to transportation, such as safety, the needs of business, the impact on communities, and the concerns of citizens. They also consider the impact of transportation systems on the environment. Increasingly, planners also look at the various elements of the transportation system—including roads, airports, harbors, and rail lines—and try to coordinate them so that they work effectively together. To prepare for the future, planners study population shifts, available energy resources, and new technologies that may offer more comfortable, convenient, or efficient ways of traveling.

Government Agencies. Transportation planning in the United States is conducted at federal, state, and local levels. The main role of the federal government is to establish policies, conduct research, supply technical assistance, and provide financial aid. The Department of Transportation has overall responsibility for federal policy. Within the department, agencies such as the Federal Highway Administration and Federal Railroad Administration focus on specific forms of transportation. The Federal Aviation Administration (FAA) approves proposals for new airports. The Bureau of Transportation Statistics, which collects and analyzes data on transportation systems, provides information to federal, state, and local planners.

State and local governments are responsible for planning and carrying out transportation projects, often based on federal guidelines. State departments of transportation and local transit authorities often work together on these projects. *See also* AIRPORTS; AIR TRAFFIC CONTROL; BART (BAY AREA RAPID TRANSIT); COMMUTING; FAA (FEDERAL AVIATION ADMINISTRATION); GOVERNMENT AND TRANSPORTATION; INTERMODAL TRANSPORT; NOISE CONTROL; POLLUTION AND TRANSPORTATION; PUBLIC TRANSPORTATION; REGULATION OF TRANSPORTATION; ROADS; TRANSPORTATION, U.S. DEPARTMENT OF; TRANSPORTATION IN THE TWENTY-FIRST CENTURY; URBAN TRANSPORTATION.

Trans-Siberian Railroad

The Trans-Siberian Railroad is the longest continuous railroad route in the world. Covering 5,778 miles (9,297 km), it runs from the Russian capital of Moscow east to the port of Vladivostok on the Sea of Japan. Travel over the entire line takes about eight days.

Czar Alexander III proposed the development of a railroad as a way to link European Russia with its territories in eastern Asia. Construction began in 1891, and the first segment opened in 1901. Passengers had to board a ferry to cross Lake Baikal in southwestern Siberia until a rail line around the lake was built several years later. In 1904 the full route from Moscow to Vladivostok was completed, but part of it ran through Manchuria. A route entirely within Russian borders was finished in 1916. The Trans-Siberian Railroad also includes the Trans-Manchurian line, which heads southeast into China, and the Trans-Mongolian line, which runs through the Mongolian capital of Ulan Bator. Another route, the Baikal Amur Mainline, crossing frozen and wet terrain to the north, opened in the 1980s. *See also* RAILROAD INDUSTRY; RAILROADS, HISTORY OF.

Travel Industry

Americans make more than one billion trips—for pleasure, business, or other reasons—each year. This vast movement of people has made the travel industry one of the most important parts of the U.S. economy. Around the world, spending on travel and tourism more than doubled during the late 1990s. The travel industry includes a wide range of companies that provide services from food and overnight accommodations to plane trips and rental cars.

Further Information
To learn more about the transportation part of the travel industry—travel by automobile, bus, airplane, train, and ship—see the related articles listed at the end of this entry.

History of the Travel Industry

Throughout history, people—including soldiers, sailors, explorers, merchants, pilgrims, refugees, and missionaries—have made journeys prompted by political, religious, economic, and other reasons. However, before the development of inexpensive and efficient methods of transportation in the 1800s, travel as a recreational activity was basically limited to the wealthy.

In ancient times rich Romans visited seaside resorts on the Mediterranean coast. On the way to these destinations, travelers could spend the night in elaborate camps set up by their servants or perhaps in primitive roadside inns, where they shared beds with other guests or slept in rooms with animals.

pilgrimage journey to a sacred place

During the Middle Ages, people traveled to trading centers, such as the great fair in Champagne, France. They also made religious **pilgrimages.** Along the route travelers could find food and lodging at inns. Wealthy pilgrims sometimes made journeys in groups, with transportation, meals, and overnight accommodations arranged by other people.

In the early 1400s prosperous Europeans began to travel for pleasure, often making long trips to the cultural centers of Europe. Travel—by horse, coach, boat, or ship—was still slow and difficult, and the possibility of attack by bandits added risk to the journey.

The development of railroads in the 1800s introduced an era of faster, less expensive travel. For the first time, members of the working class could afford to make long trips. In 1841 English missionary Thomas Cook organized the first group tour using the new railroads. A few years later, Cook opened the world's first travel agency, which offered escorted tours throughout Europe.

The travel industry expanded dramatically after World War II, especially in the United States. Income rose sharply, television and magazines publicized distant lands, and the growing use of automobiles and airplanes enabled people to make long trips. Today an individual can travel to almost any place on Earth and find places that provide meals and lodging along the way.

Elements of the Travel Industry

Many types of organizations, from automobile associations and gas stations to airlines and country inns, offer services and products for travelers. Professionals such as travel agents and tour guides also play an important role.

Many people and companies provide services that are part of the travel industry. Here, a travel agent helps a customer make reservations for a trip.

Pioneering Travel Agents

The idea of travel for pleasure developed slowly in the United States. The nation's first travel agency was founded in 1879 by Irvine Whitcomb and Walter Raymond of Boston. Their company offered tours to various mountain and seaside resorts in the Northeast. Over the next 25 years, travel agencies sprang up across the country. Among the best known were Ask Mr. Foster, located in most major cities. The American Express Company entered the tourist business in 1909, at first making travel reservations on railroads and ships and later acting as a tour operator to arrange excursions.

component *element or part that makes up a whole*

facilities *something built or created to serve a particular function*

Transportation Services. The most basic service of the travel industry is transportation. Among the organizations involved in air transportation are commercial airlines, airports, air taxi services, and companies offering aerial sightseeing excursions.

Most automobile trips are made by individuals in private cars, but car rentals represent an important and growing part of the travel industry. Much of the increase in car rentals is linked to the growth of air travel and the need for ground transportation once travelers arrive at their destination. Buses offer a less expensive alternative to air or rail travel, and they provide service to small cities and towns that cannot be reached by plane or train. Some bus lines offer sightseeing excursions to areas of special interest.

Travel by rail has declined sharply in the United States since the rise of the automobile and the airplane. However, in Europe and some other parts of the world trains continue to be an important method of transporting passengers. The fast, modern Eurail system serves some 30,000 European towns and cities.

Although large ocean liners no longer take passengers across the Atlantic on a regular basis, cruise ships still carry travelers on the high seas and other waterways. Cruises offer vacations to places such as Mexico, the Caribbean, and the Greek islands that combine travel and sightseeing with onboard entertainment.

Hospitality and Tourist Services. The hospitality **component** of the travel industry supplies food, lodging, and entertainment. A wide variety of establishments, ranging from streetside vendors, diners, and simple cafés to exclusive restaurants, provide food and drink to tourists, vacationers, and people on business trips.

Travelers can economize by staying in campgrounds, budget-priced motels, or bed-and-breakfasts, or they can splurge on luxury hotels offering first-class accommodations and service or resorts with a broad array of activities. Nightclubs, theaters, and casinos also provide entertainment for travelers.

Many people visit an area because of tourist attractions such as national parks, museums, historic sites, sports or recreation **facilities,** and theme parks. Others are drawn by special events such as the Mardi Gras, concerts, and rodeos. National parks and theme parks offer their own services for visitors, including lodging or campsites and restaurants.

Travel Companies and Professionals. The popularity of travel has given birth to a wide range of businesses and professions. Among the most important are travel agents. They act as consultants, giving clients advice on destinations and accommodations and making arrangements for their plane tickets, car rentals, hotels, cruises, or tours.

Tour operators offer travel packages that may include transportation, lodging, meals, and sightseeing. Tour escorts and travel hosts take care of the needs of travelers on package tours, attending to details such as luggage, restaurant reservations, money changing, and finding medical assistance if necessary. Tour guides lead sightseeing visits to local attractions,

Cruise ships, such as the one in this photo, provide travelers with sightseeing, entertainment, and transportation.

often providing background information on the history, art, and architecture of the place.

Computerization has revolutionized the travel industry by providing easy access to travel-related information. Companies—and travelers—can now choose between using a travel agent or making their own reservations online.

These changes have combined with continued growth to make travel one of the most dynamic industries in the United States. Americans spend more than $400 billion on travel within the country each year, and this total is expected to increase steadily. *See also* AIRLINE INDUSTRY; AMTRAK; AUTOMOBILE CLUBS; AUTOMOBILES: RELATED INDUSTRIES; BUSES; CAREERS IN TRANSPORTATION; COOK, THOMAS; CRUISE SHIPS; DRIVE-INS; EURAIL SYSTEM; FERRIES; HIGH-SPEED TRAINS; MOTELS; OCEAN LINERS; PASSENGERS; ROADS; SERVICE STATIONS; TAXIS; TOURISM.

Travel Writing

Since ancient times travelers who have visited the far places of the Earth have written accounts of their journeys to entertain, astound, and inform other people. Unlike literary tales of fictional or invented voyages, travel writing deals with real journeys.

With more people traveling than ever before, modern readers remain fascinated by the journeys of others. Nearly every bookstore has a section devoted to travel writing, and articles about travel appear in many magazines and newspapers. Some travel writing focuses on the traveler's insights, experiences, and thoughts. Other works are concerned with presenting factual descriptions and useful information.

Travel Writing Before 1700. The ancient Greeks, curious about the world around them, began the study of geography. Some of the Greek geographers were travelers who wrote about their own journeys. Strabo and Pausanias, for example, produced travel books before A.D. 200.

Trade had linked East Asia and the Mediterranean world as early as Roman times, but in the mid-1200s the vast region between the Black Sea and the Pacific Ocean came under the rule of a single state, the Mongol Empire. For the first time, Europeans could travel overland to the easternmost reaches of Asia in relative safety. Italian missionaries did so, and some of them wrote about their experiences. The best-known and most influential European traveler in Asia, however, was not a missionary. He was a Venetian merchant named Marco Polo who, with his father and uncle, spent 17 years living in the Mongol Empire. Upon returning to Italy he dictated a book from his notes.

Marco Polo's *Travels* was the most widely read travel book of its time—perhaps of all time. Its accounts of the goods in Asian markets sparked European interest in trade routes to the East. Christopher Columbus owned a well-read copy of the book and believed that he had sailed to places Marco Polo had described. But Europeans of the time knew little about the writings of Ibn Batutta, an Arab whose travels through the Muslim world in the mid-1300s covered some 75,000 miles (120,675 km), far surpassing Polo.

The European voyages of exploration that began in the 1400s launched a new wave of books about the lands visited by the explorers. In the 1500s Italian geographer Giovanni Battista Ramusio collected the writings of many previous travelers in a work called *Some Voyages and Travels,* which had volumes on Africa, America, and Asia. A few years later, England's Richard Hakluyt published *Principal Navigations, Voyages, and Discoveries of the English Nation,* an account of early English expeditions to North America.

Travel Writing Since 1700. Exploration continued to produce travel books. Georg Forster's *A Voyage Round the World* (1777) brought literary polish to travel writing and helped make such works highly popular. James Bruce's *Travels to Discover the Source of the Nile* (1790), which described its author's journey to Ethiopia, for a time was suspected of being fiction. Richard Burton's travels took him to Asia, Africa, and North and South America. After posing as a pilgrim to visit two sacred Muslim sites, he wrote *Personal Narrative of a Pilgrimage to*

Coronado's Journey to New Mexico

"The province of Quivira is 950 leagues from Mexico. Where I reached it, it is in the fortieth degree. The country itself is the best I have ever seen for producing all the products of Spain, for besides the land itself being very fat and black and being very well watered by the rivulets and springs and rivers, I found prunes like those of Spain and nuts and very good sweet grapes and mulberries. I have treated the natives of this province, and all the others whom I found wherever I went, as well as was possible, agreeably to what Your Majesty had commanded, and they have received no harm in any way from me or from those who went in my company." [Francisco Vásquez de Coronado, report to the King of Spain, 1541]

El-Medinah and Mecca (1855). Charles Montagu Doughty's *Travels in Arabia Deserta* (1888), an account of journeys in remote deserts, came to be prized for its haunting style as well as the geographic information it contained.

In the late 1700s a literary movement called Romanticism gave rise to a new kind of travel writing. The Romantics were interested in the traveler's emotional response to grand and picturesque scenery. German Romantic Goethe, who wrote about a journey to Italy, was influential in giving travel writers a new focus. Travel writing began to be more than simply an account of places visited. Writers described their reactions to what they saw, interpreted scenes for their readers, and meditated on the differences and similarities among peoples and places. Such works include Henry James's *Transatlantic Sketches* (1875), D. H. Lawrence's writings on Italy, and Hermann Keyserling's *The Travel Diary of a Philosopher* (1919).

Much travel literature about the American West was Romantic in tone. Writers played up the idea of a magnificent wilderness and its lonely heroes. Washington Irving captured the Romantic approach when he compared western landscapes to the grand and glorious cathedrals and castles of Europe.

Much modern travel writing deals with both the journey itself and the writer's inner journey of self-exploration. Among the significant travel writers of the later 1900s were Edward Hoagland, who wrote about nature and wildlife as well as travel; V. S. Naipaul, author of three noted travel books that he described as "about myself as much as India"; and Paul Theroux, whose best-selling books *The Great Railway Bazaar* (1975) and *The Old Patagonian Express* (1979) described train trips through Asia and South America.

Writers such as John Ruskin, D. H. Lawrence, Barbara Grizzuti Harrison, Mary McCarthy, and Frances Mayes have written accounts of their travels in the cities and countryside of Italy.

In addition to the literary travel narrative or travel essay, another kind of travel writing flourishes in the age of mass tourism. It is the guidebook, a collection of practical information about routes, places to stay, and things to see and do. Marco Polo presented some of the same kind of information in his *Travels,* but modern guidebooks are far more detailed and specific. They cover everything from individual cities to entire continents and are geared to all interests and all types of travelers, from student backpackers to passengers on luxury cruises. *See also* LITERATURE.

Trawlers

see Fishing Boats.

Trolleys

see Buses; Light Rail Systems.

Trucking Industry

The trucking industry provides a vital link in the economic chain. Trucks transport goods from factories and farms to distribution centers, to stores, and directly to users. About 25 percent of all intercity freight in the United States—and nearly all local freight—moves by truck.

History of Trucking.   In the early 1900s, trucks were little more than automobiles modified to carry cargo. They were too small and unreliable to function efficiently on long-distance routes. Typically, the truck itself weighed more than the cargo it carried. In addition, the poor condition of roads limited the growth of truck traffic. For these reasons, trucks were only used locally or to carry goods to and from train depots. Railroads dominated intercity freight service.

The role of trucks in commercial transportation changed during World War I. The U.S. government depended heavily on the railroads to deliver military supplies to Eastern ports. However, the volume of traffic soon overwhelmed the railroads, and trucks were used to transport cargo to drop-off points near train depots. Eventually, trucks became major freight carriers. The number of trucks increased dramatically during the war, and businesses soon recognized their value for hauling smaller loads. Trucks could transport freight door-to-door, eliminating the need for storing goods at depots. They also provided service to small communities that were not on railroad lines.

Trucking grew dramatically during the 1920s, and by the 1930s long-distance trucking became an important method of shipping goods. Anyone who owned a truck could carry freight. However, some operated unsafe trucks or dangerously overloaded their vehicles. Heavy competition from larger companies drove many small operators out of business. The Motor Carrier Act of 1935 was passed to address these problems by regulating trucking companies. Under the act, control of the trucking industry was assigned to the Interstate Commerce Commission (ICC). The ICC determined which companies could enter the industry and specified the services a carrier could provide and the rates it could charge. In addition, applicants for trucking licenses were required to prove that their services were needed by the public.

The trucking industry flourished during and after World War II, becoming a major competitor for railroads. The development of tractor trailers increased the freight capacity of trucks. The federal government standardized weight limits for trucks, which made it easier to transport cargo across state lines. The percentage of freight hauled by the railroads declined steadily as trucks moved more and more of the nation's goods. Trucks offered a more efficient way of transporting lightweight or fragile goods between factories and shops and warehouses.

As the importance of trucking continued to increase in the 1970s, many people called for an end to regulation to allow more carriers in the industry. The Motor Carrier Act of 1980 deregulated the trucking industry, eliminating regulation of rates and permitting existing companies to expand their routes and new companies to form. In the six years following passage of the act, 32,000 new carriers were licensed. The response to **deregulation** has been mixed: some people feel it has benefited the industry by forcing trucking companies to become more efficient, while others argue that increased competition has hurt independent truckers. In 1996 Congress abolished the ICC, and many of its responsibilities relating to motor vehicles passed to the Department of Transportation.

deregulation *process of removing restrictions and regulations*

Structure of the Trucking Industry.

There are two basic kinds of trucking firms: private carriers and public, or for-hire, carriers. A private carrier is a large business that maintains a fleet of trucks for its own use.

For-hire carriers offer their services to customers for a fee. One type, known as contract carriers, transports goods for particular firms according to the terms of a contract. The other type, common carriers, serve the general public. Drivers for common carriers may be salaried employees of the carrier or independent owner-operators.

Regardless of the type of carrier, the shipping of goods by truck is subject to federal and state regulations, including weight limits and safety standards. The Federal Highway Administration and the Surface Transportation Board, both at the U.S. Department of Transportation, issue and enforce many rules relating to interstate motor carriers. State laws regulate shipments within a state.

Trucks may carry two kinds of shipments: truckload (TL) and less than truckload (LTL). A TL shipment refers to the pickup and delivery of an entire load directly to a single location. LTL shipping involves picking up several small loads and delivering them to different locations. Because small loads require many different stops and more time and labor to load and unload, LTL shipping is less efficient and more expensive than TL shipping.

To promote safe driving, federal laws limit the number of hours truck drivers may work and require rest periods. These regulations affect company schedules and delivery deadlines. The need for drivers to rest on long-distance routes has given rise to private truck stops, roadside

Lumpers Unload

Because of tight delivery schedules and limits on the number of hours of work, truck drivers often rely on people known as lumpers to unload their vehicles. Trucking companies generally pay for lumpers to help their drivers. But independent owner-operators who use lumpers must pay for the service themselves. The expression "If you don't like it you can lump it" may have come from these "lumpers."

The trucking industry carries freight quickly and efficiently across cities and countries.

facilities something built or created to serve a particular function

facilities on highways that include a restaurant, fuel pumps, and a spacious parking area for trucks. Public rest stops with the same facilities often provide separate parking for trucks. *See also* Delivery Services; Freight; Government and Transportation; Interstate Commerce Commission; Moving and Storage; Regulation of Transportation; Trade and Commerce; Transportation, U.S. Department of; Trucks.

Trucks

Trucks—from pickups and dump trucks to tractor trailer rigs—are used to haul goods from place to place. Most large trucks provide transportation for commercial freight. Small trucks generally serve as vehicles for deliveries, carrying equipment and materials, or personal travel. The sales of pickups, vans, and other light trucks have increased dramatically in recent years, as models with comfortable interiors have become popular passenger vehicles.

The Development of Trucks

The world's first truck was produced in 1896 by the German auto manufacturer Gottlieb Daimler. It featured a 4-horsepower engine and a transmission with two forward gears and one reverse gear. Two years later the Winton Company introduced the first American-made truck, which was equipped with a 6-horsepower engine. These early trucks could carry loads of 5 tons and had top speeds of less than 15 miles per hour (24 km per hour). The driver sat in an open cab located directly over the engine, which was powered by steam, gasoline, or electricity.

During World War I the army ordered thousands of trucks, and from 1917 to 1918 the number of trucks produced in the United States nearly doubled to almost 200,000 a year. By this time, trucks had increased in size up to 15 tons, and many roads built to handle lighter automobiles crumbled under the weight of heavy truck traffic.

Technological Improvements. In the 1920s trucks became larger, more powerful, and more complex. Bigger engines increased the load a truck could haul. Transmissions with as many as seven forward gears replaced the chain-drive system of early trucks and gave the driver greater control. Air-filled tires replaced solid steel or solid rubber tires, and air braking systems made stopping a fully loaded truck easier and safer. The tractor trailer—a powered cab that towed a separate trailer—had appeared on the road a few years earlier.

One of the most important developments in trucking was the introduction of diesel engines. More powerful and fuel-efficient than gasoline engines, diesels allowed trucks to haul heavier loads at faster speeds

This drawing shows the major parts of a tractor trailer.

Parts of a Tractor Trailer

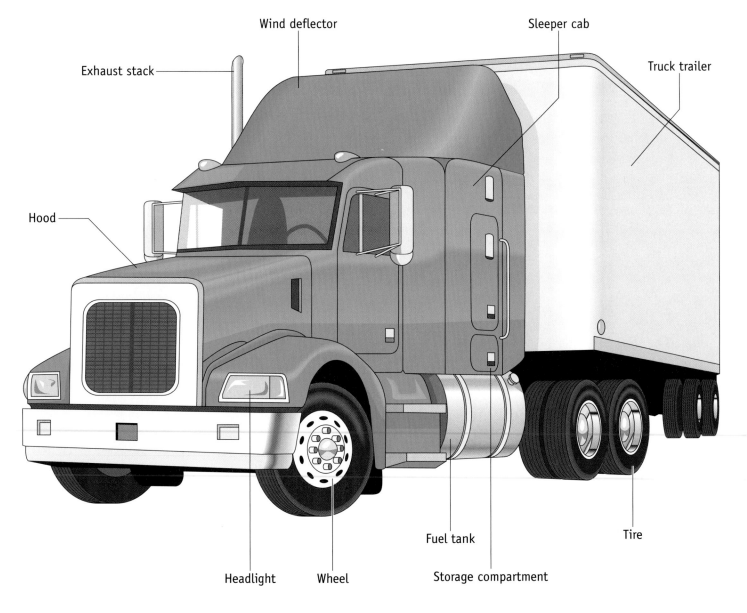

while cutting fuel costs nearly in half. The truck's ability to deliver goods inexpensively to any destination produced a trucking boom during the 1920s. By 1925 there were some 2.5 million trucks on U.S. roads. The improvement of roads during these years was a major factor in the growth of trucking.

Further Advances. World War II saw further advances in truck design, including more powerful diesel engines, power steering, and all-wheel drive for traveling over rugged terrain. After the war, manufacturers made ever larger trucks. They also adjusted the shape and materials of the vehicles to decrease wind resistance, increase fuel efficiency, and reduce weight. Some new trucks had sleeper cabs to allow drivers to take quick naps and avoid the expense of hotel rooms on long hauls. A crew of two drivers could take turns resting and driving the truck.

Modern trucks may include various features to make driving safer and increase the efficiency of deliveries. Electronic sensors alert drivers when they are close to other vehicles or when a vehicle is in the truck's blind spot. Some systems even automatically slow the truck down to keep it at a safe distance from vehicles ahead of it. Onboard computers note the average speed of a truck, how close it comes to other vehicles, how often it brakes, and other data to allow company officials to monitor the driving habits of individual truckers. The satellite-based Global Positioning System (GPS) can determine the exact location of a truck, and onboard E-mail keeps drivers in touch with company headquarters.

Types of Trucks

Trucks are used for a variety of jobs, including hauling freight, towing, fire fighting, and construction. However, trucks are generally categorized not by function but by size and weight.

Heavy trucks, such as the combination rig shown here, are used to transport large loads of freight.

Truck Classifications. There are three general categories of trucks: light straight trucks, medium straight trucks, and heavy trucks. A "straight" truck is a single-unit vehicle that does not pull a trailer. A truck made up of more than one unit, such as a cab and trailer, is called an "articulated" or "combination" truck.

By far the most common type of truck is the light straight truck. These vehicles weigh less than 14,000 pounds (6,360 kg) when fully loaded, which is known as their gross vehicle weight. They include pickup trucks and vans. More than 90 percent of all trucks in the United States are light trucks.

Medium straight trucks are used mainly for local transportation, but they sometimes carry freight on long-distance routes. These trucks have a gross vehicle weight that ranges from 14,000 to 33,000 pounds (6,360 to 14,980 kg).

Heavy trucks, with a gross vehicle weight over 33,000 pounds (14,980 kg), may be straight trucks or combination rigs. The truck cab, or tractor, in a combination rig may pull either a full trailer or a semitrailer. A full trailer rolls on wheels that support all of its weight. The front end of a semitrailer rests on the tractor, which supports part of the semitrailer's weight. Medium and heavy trucks each make up about 4 percent of all truck sales.

Special Kinds of Trucks. Many trucks are specially designed to perform a particular job. Emergency vehicles, such as ambulances and fire engines, are built on truck bodies modified to include the equipment used by rescue crews and firefighters. Recreational vehicles often consist of single-unit trucks or trailers equipped with living accommodations. Construction trucks such as dump trucks and cement mixers are designed to move certain types of materials to and from building sites.

Some freight trucks are specially suited for carrying particular goods, with refrigerated or heated cargo areas, tanks for transporting liquids, or a flatbed for vehicles or machinery. With the increase in **containerization,** many trucks are equipped to haul large fully loaded containers that can be transferred to ships or railcars. *See also* CONTAINERIZATION; DAIMLER, GOTTLIEB; DRIVING; EMERGENCY TRANSPORTATION; ENGINES; FIRE ENGINES; FREIGHT; INTERMODAL TRANSPORT; RECREATIONAL VEHICLES (RVS); SPORT UTILITY VEHICLES; TRUCKING INDUSTRY; VANS AND MINIVANS.

Tough as a Bulldog

One of the most recognizable truck brands in the United States is the Mack truck, known by its bulldog mascot. The inspiration for the mascot came from British engineers in World War I, who called the Mack truck "the bulldog" because of its rugged appearance. The name stuck and became the company symbol. A sheet metal plate showing a bulldog with the word *Mack* printed on its collar was riveted to each side of the trucks. The Mack trucks that were so popular in the war were also used in many major construction projects.

containerization method of shipping cargo in boxlike containers that can be transferred from one type of transportation to another

Tsiolkovsky, Konstantin
Russian rocket pioneer

Konstantin Tsiolkovsky (1857–1935) developed many of the basic ideas that made space travel possible. He published various works on spaceflight, including a 1903 paper on the use of rockets in space. Tsiolkovsky realized that rockets were the only type of engine both powerful enough to propel a spacecraft and capable of functioning in the airless atmosphere of space. He recommended that liquid fuels rather than solid fuels be used in early rockets.

Tsiolkovsky studied the problems of space travel, such as how to protect astronauts from the rapid acceleration during launch and the harsh conditions of space and how to control the reentry of spacecraft into

This crater on the Moon was named after Konstantin Tsiolkovsky, a pioneer in the field of rocket engineering and spaceflight.

Earth's atmosphere. The idea of multistage rockets, later used in many launch vehicles, also came from Tsiolkovsky. *See also* ROCKETS; SPACE EXPLORATION; SPACE TRAVEL.

Tugboats

A tugboat is a small, powerful ship used to push or tow larger vessels. The three basic types of tugboats—harbor tugs, oceangoing tugs, and river tugs—have different functions. Harbor tugs guide large ships into or out of harbors. Oceangoing tugs tow disabled ships into port or tow ships or structures such as floating docks across the open sea. River tugs are used to push long strings of unpowered ships called barges along rivers or other inland waterways.

Scottish engineer William Symington built the first tugboat in 1802. Called the *Charlotte Dundas,* it was a paddle-wheel vessel powered by a Watt steam engine. In 1815 the steamship *Enterprise* towed a ship from the Gulf of Mexico up the Mississippi River to New Orleans, making it the first tug to be used for commercial purposes. Commercial towing began in England the following year, when the steam-powered *Majestic* pulled a ship on the Thames River. England's Royal Navy soon acquired two steamships to tow large warships out of the harbor when wind conditions prevented them from moving under sail power.

Early tugs were driven by side-mounted paddle wheels. By the 1850s screw propellers were replacing paddle wheels as the means of powering tugboats, and by 1900 diesel engines were introduced.

Tugboats are used to push or tow larger vessels in harbors, oceans, and rivers. Here, a tugboat crosses New York Harbor.

Modern tugboats are much more powerful, though not significantly larger, than the vessels of the 1800s. The typical harbor tug weighs about 250 tons, and its diesel engines can generate some 2,500 horsepower. Oceangoing tugs, which sail in the deeper and rougher waters of the open sea, weigh up to 2,000 tons and can generate 15,000 to 20,000 horsepower.

Tugboats either push or pull the ships they are guiding. European tugs are more likely to pull vessels than to push them. In the United States, tugs usually push on the bow, stern, or sides of the vessels they tow. Pulling tugboats have special equipment that automatically adjusts tow lines, preventing the lines from falling into the water and becoming tangled in the vessel's propellers. The bows of pushing tugs have been reinforced to withstand the stress of pushing large ships. The bows of river tugs are designed to fit into notches on the stern of the barge they push. River tugs can move up to 40 barges linked together, a load that is longer than the world's largest ocean liner. *See also* BARGES; HARBORS AND PORTS; HORSEPOWER; SHIPS AND BOATS, TYPES OF.

Tunnels

Tunnels are horizontal passageways used to carry roads, walkways, railway lines, or canals through hills and mountains or other obstacles. They may also be built below ground and under rivers or other bodies of water. Tunnels are usually created by digging through soil or rock, though some underwater tunnels consist of sections that have been constructed on land.

History of Tunnels. Many ancient civilizations built underground passageways, mainly for irrigation or sewage. The first tunnel designed for transportation was probably the 5,000-foot (1,520-m) Pausulippo tunnel, created by the Romans in 36 B.C. to connect the cities of Naples and Pozzuoli.

After Roman times, tunneling came to an almost complete halt in Europe until the start of canal construction in the 1600s. During the great age of canals between 1760 and about 1830, hundreds of canal tunnels were dug throughout Europe and the United States.

The growth of railroads led to a tremendous spurt of tunnel construction from the mid-1800s to early 1900s. Many railroad tunnels were built in Europe. The Allegheny Portage Railroad completed the first American rail tunnel in 1833.

The construction of railroad tunnels gave rise to new techniques and equipment, including the use of explosives for blasting through rock and the development of powerful drills for cutting into rock. Better tools and methods greatly increased the speed and ease of tunneling and made it possible to build much longer tunnels. The 12.3-mile (19.8-km) Simplon Tunnel in the Alps, built between 1898 and 1906, was the longest tunnel in the world for many years.

In the late 1800s, several cities around the world built subway tunnels beneath their streets. A big surge in tunnel construction came with the growth of automobile traffic in the 1920s. The first great underwater tunnel for motor vehicles, the Holland Tunnel, opened in 1927. Running under the Hudson River between New Jersey and New York City, it introduced a powerful ventilation system with huge fans in towers at either end of the tunnel to exhaust stale air and draw in fresh air.

Since World War II, tunnels have become increasingly longer and larger. The Channel Tunnel, over 30 miles (48 km) in length, runs under the English Channel linking France and England. Even longer is the 33.6-mile (54.1-km) Seikan railroad tunnel in Japan.

Tunnel Construction. Early tunnel building was a slow and difficult process. Workers split rock by hand using simple hammers and saws. They also used fire to heat rock and then cooled it quickly with water, causing the rock to crack. These methods were used to make tunnels until the introduction of gunpowder in the 1600s.

Workers often use explosives and drills to dig through rock to build tunnels.

Gunpowder and other explosives soon became basic tools of tunnel building, especially for passageways through hard rock. Workers drilled holes into the rock face and filled them with explosives. When the explosives were ignited, the resulting blast shattered the rock. Workers would then clear away the rubble. Modern tunnel builders still drill and blast to cut through hard rock, generally using dynamite and a movable platform called a jumbo on which many drills are mounted.

Until the 1800s building tunnels through soft rock, clay, and soil was difficult because these materials collapsed too easily. This changed with the invention of the shield, a rigid, cylinder-shaped frame that supports the soil while workers dig forward. As the shield moves ahead, loosened rock and debris pass through openings in it and are carried away. Metal sections are then bolted in place inside the rear of the shield, forming a solid lining that may be later covered with concrete. When tunneling through soft or wet soil, compressed air is pumped into the tunnel and the air pressure at the digging site helps keep the surrounding soil from collapsing. Workers enter and exit the tunnel through an airtight chamber known as an air lock.

Large automated tunnel-boring machines called moles are also used, especially when drilling through medium-hard rock. Moles contain many sharp, rotating cutting heads that crush the rock, eliminating the need for blasting. The machines are capable of digging up to several hundred feet of tunnel per day.

prefabricated *manufactured in advance*

Shields and compressed air have often been used to build underwater tunnels. Another common method involves **prefabricated** steel tunnel sections, sealed at each end, that are lowered into trenches at the bottom of a body of water. When the sections are in place, divers connect them and cover them with fill. Workers then enter from either end to cut away the dividers that seal the sections and to finish work on the inside of the tunnel. *See also* AQUEDUCTS; CANALS; CHANNEL TUNNEL; RAILROAD INDUSTRY; SUBWAYS.

TWA

see Airline Industry.

U-Boats

see Submarines and Submersibles.

Unions

see Labor Unions.

Urban Transportation

Urban transportation, also known as mass transit, refers to the various forms of transportation—such as buses, subways, trolleys, commuter trains, and taxis—that carry people throughout a city and its suburbs. Mass transit is vital to the growth and economic well-being of metropolitan regions. It has also greatly influenced the shape and structure of cities.

History of Urban Transportation

When walking or riding animals were the only forms of transportation, cities remained small. Cities began to expand as transportation improved, allowing people to travel farther in less time.

By 1828 private companies in Paris were operating large horse-drawn carriages called omnibuses, some of which could carry as many as 50 people. The vehicles traveled along the busiest routes so that they could serve as many passengers as possible at all times. This principle has remained a basic feature of mass transit up to the present day.

In 1832 omnibus operators in New York City installed rails in the streets, which made the ride smoother and enabled the horses to pull heavier loads. These vehicles became known as streetcars. Soon a number of large cities had rail-based streetcar systems. By the mid-1800s, however, steam locomotives had replaced horses in urban rail systems. Later, steam gave way to electric power, which is still used for powering modern subways and trolleys.

To increase the speed of service, some cities moved rail lines away from road traffic. Some were elevated above the city streets, and others were placed in tunnels below. New York built the first elevated urban rail line in 1868. The first subway opened in London in 1863, and by the early 1900s cities such as Boston, New York, and Paris had subways as well. Cities were already using motorized buses to carry passengers along routes not served by rail lines.

After the number of automobiles on the road soared in the 1920s, the use of mass transit declined. Cars gave people the freedom to go anywhere, any time—something urban transportation systems could not do. The increase of car ownership also contributed to a dramatic growth of suburbs. Suburban residents could commute to work in the cities by car instead of by mass transit. By the 1970s the ridership on mass transit systems in the United States had dropped to about one-third of the level of the 1920s.

Urban mass transit has had more success in other countries. In Europe, the cost of owning and operating an automobile is much greater than in the United States, and European governments have generally spent more money for mass transit than for highways. Mass transit also remains popular in many developing countries, where few people can afford to own cars.

Urban Transportation Today

Mass transit is still an important part of the life of modern cities. In the past most urban mass transit systems were privately owned, but today governments control their planning and funding.

Urban Transportation Services. Modern urban transportation falls into two categories: fixed-route and flexible. Fixed-route services—such as subways, trolleys, light rail systems, and commuter trains—must follow predetermined routes. Power is provided by a third

Moving Crowds of Commuters

The Japanese city of Tokyo has one of the most heavily used mass transit systems in the world. Riding the subway is inexpensive and extremely popular. Although the subways run frequently, they become so crowded during rush hours that employees push people on board to fill the cars and allow the doors to close. The railroad line that runs through Tokyo also floods with people at rush hour. To handle the crowds, new cars on the busy Yamanote line were designed with as many doors as possible.

rail or overhead electric lines along the route. These transit systems run on regular schedules, usually travel along main thoroughfares, and can carry many passengers. A typical subway train, for example, can transport about 14,000 people an hour. In the same period, motor vehicles in a lane of traffic on a highway could move only about 5,000 people.

Subways and trolleys generally operate within a city. Commuter trains often serve as links between the city and outlying suburbs. High-speed trains, capable of traveling more than 100 miles (161 km) per hour, can connect cities—such as Washington, D.C., and Baltimore—that are some distance apart. Often separated from other traffic, fixed-route services are fast and efficient but inflexible.

Flexible services include buses, taxis, and other vehicles that travel freely along streets and highways. Some flexible services, such as buses, run on fixed schedules; others, such as taxis, offer unscheduled service. Airport shuttles and dial-a-ride vans that provide transportation for the elderly and people with disabilities are also in the flexible services category. For-hire transportation services that carry only a few passengers are known as paratransit.

Flexible transportation services offer convenience. They can change routes and schedules easily and can serve many more locations than fixed-route services. However, flexible services are generally much slower than those on fixed routes, mainly because of traffic delays and frequent stops to pick up and unload passengers. In addition, flexible services add more vehicles to the flow of traffic, contributing to the crowding of streets and increased air pollution.

Operations and Funding. Although passengers must pay to use almost all forms of urban mass transit, their fares rarely cover the cost of operations. Even on the most successful and heavily used systems, the fares pay only about 70 percent of operating expenses.

The remainder of the funds needed to operate urban transportation systems comes from taxpayers. The U.S. federal government has been involved in the financing of mass transit since 1964, but state and city governments provide a larger share of the public funds. In Europe and many other parts of the world, urban transportation systems receive large amounts of money from the national government.

Government funding is necessary because of the high cost of operating mass transit systems. Fixed-route services are very expensive to build because of the need to install rails, construct stations, and purchase costly vehicles and equipment. Setting up a bus system requires less of an investment, but the operating costs may be higher than those of a light rail or subway system. One reason is that each additional bus needs a driver, whereas new subway cars can be added to an existing train without hiring new employees.

Another factor affecting the cost of mass transit is that the systems are used lightly for much of the day.

Buses play a major role in the urban transportation systems of many cities. This electric-powered bus carries passengers in Oxford, England.

Passenger ferries often serve commuters as well as recreational travelers. The ferry shown here crosses Elliott Bay near Seattle, Washington.

Nevertheless, a full fleet of buses, trains, subways, and other vehicles must be available to meet demand during rush hours or other periods of peak ridership. Mass transit systems try to deal with these variations in passenger traffic by providing less frequent service during off-peak hours. They may also offer lower fares at these times to encourage more people to use mass transit during slow periods.

Impact on Cities. Cities need affordable and reliable mass transit to prosper and grow. Many city dwellers do not own cars, and those who do often cannot find reasonably priced parking in urban centers. They rely on mass transit to travel to schools, work, stores, entertainment, and various social activities. Likewise, urban businesses depend on mass transit to bring them customers and employees. Commuter trains make it possible for people who work in cities to live in distant suburbs and for city residents to commute to jobs in the suburbs.

Besides its economic effects, urban transportation has a major impact on the quality of life in a city. Mass transit helps decrease the number of automobiles on the street, which reduces air pollution and relieves traffic congestion. It also reduces the need for parking, which allows land to be used for more productive purposes, such as apartment houses, office buildings, hospitals, shops, or museums and other cultural centers. In addition, urban mass transit allows a greater number of people to live, work, and spend their leisure time in the city, which strengthens the city's economy and cultural life. It enables students, the elderly, and people with physical disabilities to enjoy many of the city's benefits. *See also* Buses; Cable Cars and Funiculars; Commuting; Government and Transportation; High-Speed Trains; Light Rail Systems; Passengers; People Movers; Public Transportation; Subways; Taxis; Transportation Planning.

Vans and Minivans

A van is an enclosed truck used for transporting goods or people. A minivan is a smaller version of the van, designed solely as a passenger vehicle. The ample passenger space available in vans and minivans has made them among the most popular types of family vehicles in the United States.

Vans. The earliest vans, called panel trucks, were working vehicles used for deliveries and for hauling tools and equipment. William Stout, an aircraft designer, created a passenger van called the Scarab in the early 1930s. This beetle-shaped vehicle, described as a "living room on wheels," featured a spacious interior, movable seats, and a fold-down table. However, the Scarab made its appearance during the Great Depression and did not sell well.

Meanwhile, vans gradually attracted a following in Europe. Smaller than pickup trucks, they could haul heavy loads through narrow European streets. Vans also got better gas mileage than trucks, an important selling point because gas was very expensive in Europe.

The first van to become popular in the United States was the Volkswagen, imported from Germany in the 1950s. Chevrolet then introduced a van, and Ford and Dodge followed with their own models. The popularity of

With ample space for passengers, bikes, and luggage, minivans became popular family vehicles in the 1980s and 1990s.

vans grew in the 1960s, particularly among young people who bought and fixed up old delivery vans. They often decorated the exteriors with colorful scenes and designs and outfitted the interiors with carpeting and stereos. The van came to be a symbol of the free lifestyle of the youth culture of the 1960s and 1970s. Later, manufacturers began to build custom vans that offered luxurious interiors.

Minivans. The image of the van changed in 1983 when Chrysler introduced the minivan, a smaller version of the van. Designed as a family vehicle, the minivan was an immediate success and rapidly took over the market once dominated by the station wagon. Minivans became the vehicle of choice for families who needed room to haul children, pets, groceries, and hobby and sports equipment. Within a few years, nearly every American carmaker was producing minivans, as were many foreign manufacturers.

Minivans offer abundant cargo space and movable—or removable—seats to allow owners to transport large or bulky items. Luxury features such as videocassette players and power-operated sliding doors have been added to increase the vehicles' comfort and convenience. Sport utility vehicles (SUVs), which became popular in the 1990s, have taken away some of the market for minivans. But minivans continue to have a loyal following in the United States. *See also* Automobiles, Types of; Recreational Vehicles (RVs); Sport Utility Vehicles; Trucks.

Viaducts

A viaduct is a bridge that is often made up of a series of arches supported by high towers, or piers. Viaducts are typically used to carry a road or railway over other roads, valleys, or bodies of water. The ancient Romans built the earliest viaducts, including the Alcántara in Spain that dates from A.D. 98.

For nearly 2,000 years, most viaducts were constructed from stone or masonry. However, many railroad viaducts of the 1800s were made of wood and later iron or steel. Most modern viaducts are built with steel-reinforced concrete. The Tunkhannock Viaduct near Scranton, Pennsylvania, is one of the largest concrete-and-steel railroad viaducts in the world. Built between 1912 and 1915, it is 2,375 feet (724 m) long and 240 feet (73 m) high. *See also* Bridges.

Vikings

In the years between A.D. 800 and about 1050, Vikings of northern Europe terrorized other Europeans with brutal raids and invasions. These Northmen—also known as Norsemen or Normans—excelled as shipbuilders and navigators. They also sailed forth boldly in search of empty lands to colonize in the North Atlantic Ocean, reaching North America 500 years before Columbus.

The Vikings came from Scandinavia: Sweden, Norway, and Denmark. Population growth and a shortage of available land for farming drove them from their homelands, first on seasonal raiding expeditions and later on longer excursions for trading and colonizing. In general, the

Danes headed south to Europe and the Mediterranean. The Swedes moved east into the lands around the Black Sea, where they founded the beginning of the Russian state.

The Norwegians went west, raiding and then settling the Shetland and Orkney Islands north of Scotland and the coast of Ireland. In the late 800s they began settling Iceland, and from there, in the late 900s, they launched several colonies on the shores of Greenland. Around 1000 Leif Eriksson sailed west from Greenland and landed at several points on the North American coast. Although scholars are still debating the location of the Viking settlement called Vinland, **archaeologists** have found evidence of a short-lived Viking colony on the island of Newfoundland.

The Vikings' success was due in part to their well-made, **maneuverable** ships. For coastal raiding and shipping they used longships, long, shallow vessels that could glide onto beaches and sail up rivers. For voyages in the open sea they used the halfship, or *knorr,* a shorter, broader vessel with higher sides and greater cargo capacity than the longship. Both types of Viking ships carried sails as well as oars. *See also* SAILBOATS AND SAILING SHIPS; SHIPS AND BOATS.

archaeologist *scientist who studies past human cultures, usually by digging up ruins*

maneuverable *able to make a series of changes in course easily*

Viking Space Probes

probe *uncrewed spacecraft sent out to explore and collect information in space*

Two U.S. Viking space **probes** explored Mars in the 1970s and early 1980s. *Viking 1* was launched on August 20, 1975, about three weeks before *Viking 2* lifted off. The two craft landed on Mars about 4,000 miles (6,436 km) apart, almost a year after leaving Earth.

Both Viking probes consisted of two parts: an orbiter and a lander. The orbiters circled Mars and photographed its surface to select suitable landing sites. Then the landers separated from the orbiters and, by opening parachutes and firing small rockets, slowed down to make a soft landing on the planet.

The landers performed a series of scientific experiments on Mars. They analyzed the Martian soil, wind, and atmosphere and transmitted close-up photographs of Mars to Earth. They also scooped up soil samples and tested them in tiny onboard laboratories to determine whether life was present. Meanwhile, the orbiters continued to circle the planet, studying its atmosphere and mapping its surface. They also acted as radio relay stations to transmit data collected by the landers back to Earth.

The Viking orbiters sent back data until 1980. The *Viking 1* lander ceased operation in 1978, but the *Viking 2* lander lasted until 1982, much longer than expected. Although the probes discovered no evidence of life on Mars, they sent back more than 56,000 images and paved the way for later Mars missions. *See also* MARS PROBES; SPACE EXPLORATION; SPACE PROBES.

Vintage Cars

Many people collect and restore vintage—or antique—cars, models from earlier periods that are no longer in production. Vintage automobiles are divided into categories depending on their age, though the classifications are not rigid. The oldest, those produced before 1905, are sometimes called pioneer cars. Vehicles dating from 1906 to 1912, when

Many car enthusiasts collect and restore antique cars, such as this 1939 Rover.

many of the first auto manufacturing companies were founded, are known as veteran or brass era cars. The term *vintage cars* is sometimes used to refer to automobiles built between 1913 and 1919. Classic cars, luxury models introduced between 1925 and 1942, form another group. Classic cars are large vehicles that were often custom-built. Many of them had exotic details such as ostrich leather seats or rosewood dashboards. Only the very wealthy could afford such cars when they were new. They have since become some of the most highly prized antique automobiles.

Antique car enthusiasts also collect models from later eras, such as the Ford Thunderbird and the Chevrolet Corvette. Many belong to clubs that focus on a particular make of car. *See also* AUTOMOBILE CLUBS; AUTOMOBILES, HISTORY OF.

Volkswagen

Volkswagen, one of the leading German automakers, is best known for the design of its first car, the Beetle. The name *Volkswagen* means "people's car" in German.

In 1934 the German government directed auto designer Ferdinand Porsche to develop a car that would be both reliable and affordable. Although several test vehicles were built in the next few years, the Volkswagen company itself was not founded until 1938. The company produced 630 Beetles in its Wolfsburg factory before World War II, but Allied bombing during the war destroyed much of the plant and stopped production.

After the war the Allied powers found the factory in their hands. They helped the Germans start making Beetles again, and by 1948 the company was producing more than half of the cars in Germany. A convertible and a van were soon added to the Volkswagen line. In the 1950s the company began exporting vehicles to many countries including the United States, where Volkswagens became very popular. By the early 1970s the Beetle had become the best-selling car of all time.

In the following decades, popular Volkswagen cars included the Passat, the Golf (also known in the United States as the Rabbit), and the Jetta. The New Beetle, introduced in 1998, resembled the original from the 1930s in its curved shape and compact design. Volkswagen owns several other auto companies, including Audi in Germany and SEAT in Spain. It also makes and sells cars in partnership with Fiat in Italy and Skoda in the Czech Republic. *See also* AUTOMOBILE INDUSTRY; VANS AND MINIVANS.

Von Braun, Wernher
Rocket engineer

guided missile *missile, or rocket, steered by radio signals and electronic codes*

Wernher von Braun and a team of engineers developed the Saturn V rocket. In 1969 the rocket powered the Apollo spacecraft that carried the first humans to the Moon.

Wernher von Braun (1912–1977), a German-born engineer, played a key role in developing rocket and spaceflight technology. As a student, von Braun read *The Rocket to Interplanetary Space* by the German rocket pioneer Hermann Oberth. Von Braun was so frustrated that he could not understand the math in the book that he studied until he rose to the top of his class.

In the 1930s von Braun worked with Oberth testing liquid-fuel rockets. The German Army recruited von Braun to work on rocket designs, and during World War II, he and his team developed one of the early **guided missiles,** the V-2.

In 1945 von Braun surrendered to U.S. troops and came to America. With his team of engineers, he built the Redstone and Jupiter missiles

for the U.S. Army, and in 1958, with a modified Redstone, they launched the first U.S. satellite, *Explorer 1*. In 1960 von Braun's team was transferred from the army to the newly created National Aeronautics and Space Administration (NASA). His greatest achievement was the Saturn V rocket, which in 1969 launched the Apollo spacecraft that carried the first humans to the Moon. Von Braun retired from NASA in 1972 and became president of the National Space Institute, a private organization to promote understanding and support for space exploration. *See also* APOLLO PROGRAM; GUIDED MISSILES; NASA; OBERTH, HERMANN; ROCKETS; SPACE EXPLORATION.

Voyager Space Probes

probe *uncrewed spacecraft sent out to explore and collect information in space*

The two Voyager space **probes** were launched in 1977. Exploring the outer planets of the solar system, they discovered many new satellites and the existence of rings around Jupiter, Uranus, and Neptune; detected active volcanoes on one of Jupiter's moons; and witnessed major storms on Neptune and Jupiter.

Powered by small nuclear generators, the Voyager probes were specially designed for extremely long journeys. They used one planet's gravity like a slingshot to speed them on to the next one. This method of traveling, which cut the flight time to Neptune from 30 years to about 12 years, is possible only once every 176 years when the outer planets are lined up in a particular path. In addition, their communications equipment transmitted information more than 100 times faster than that of the earlier Pioneer probes.

Both Voyager probes flew by Jupiter in 1979 and sent back thousands of images of the planet and its moons. After leaving Jupiter, *Voyager 1* passed by Saturn in 1980 and explored its largest moon, Titan. It then left the solar system. *Voyager 2* reached Saturn in 1981 and continued on to Uranus in 1986 and Neptune in 1989 before heading out of the solar system.

As they travel beyond the solar system, both Voyagers will continue to transmit information back to Earth until their generators run out of power in about the year 2020. The probes carry recordings of sounds from Earth and greetings in 60 languages in case they are found by intelligent life-forms. *See also* SPACE EXPLORATION; SPACE PROBES.

Wagons

see Carts, Carriages, and Wagons.

Walking

The oldest form of human transportation is one that most people still use every day: walking. For centuries, walking was the most common method of traveling. However, many people in industrialized nations seldom go from place to place on foot. They work in offices rather than fields, they drive to most destinations, and they spend much of their leisure time sitting. To counter this lack of activity, some people make a special effort to walk for fitness and recreation.

Hiking. Walking for pleasure outdoors, also known as hiking, can take place in a variety of locations—from urban parks and "greenways" on the outskirts of cities to trails in national forests and wilderness areas. Hikers walk alone or in groups. They often wear sturdy boots and carry packs holding water and gear. Fitness experts recommend hiking as an excellent form of exercise.

Many people enjoy hiking for its own sake. Others hike as part of outdoor activities such as mountain climbing, hunting, and **orienteering.** Overnight hiking trips, also called backpacking, combine hiking with camping. Clubs and conservation associations in the United States, Europe, and elsewhere organize group hikes.

orienteering sport that involves navigating across the countryside using a map or compass

Racewalking. Competitive speed walking, or racewalking, originated in the second half of the 1800s. In 1866 the Amateur Athletic Club of England introduced a 7-mile (11-km) walking race. Round-the-clock walking races took place on indoor tracks in New York during the 1870s and 1880s. The events lasted six days, during which competitors could take breaks to eat, rest, and nap.

In 1908 men's racewalking events of 3,500 meters and 10 miles (16 km) were added to the Olympic Games. By 1992 the Olympics included 20- and 50-kilometer race walks for men and a 10-kilometer walk for women.

Racewalking is not simply a fast stride. The form of the stride is also important. A racewalker's forward-moving foot touches the ground before the rear foot leaves the ground, and the forward leg remains straight as it passes under the body. Racewalkers also bend their arms and swing their hands as they move.

People who walk, hike, or race walk can lose weight and improve the functioning of their heart, lungs, and circulatory system. Taking a route that includes hills adds to the workout. *See also* MOUNTAINEERING; SPORTS AND RECREATION; TRAILS.

Wankel, Felix

see Engines.

Water Currents, Tides, and Waves

Anyone who has ever traveled on oceans, lakes, or rivers knows that these bodies of water do not stand still. Travel by water is movement on a surface that is also in motion. An understanding of the main types of water motion—currents, tides, and waves—is important because they can affect a vessel's safety, speed, and ability to hold a steady course.

Currents. Any horizontal flow of water is a current. Rivers and streams, which move gradually downhill through channels on the Earth's surface, are currents. Similar currents flow within oceans, seas, and large lakes.

The world's oceans are filled with patterns of currents, some moving in one direction, others sweeping around in vast circles. Two of the

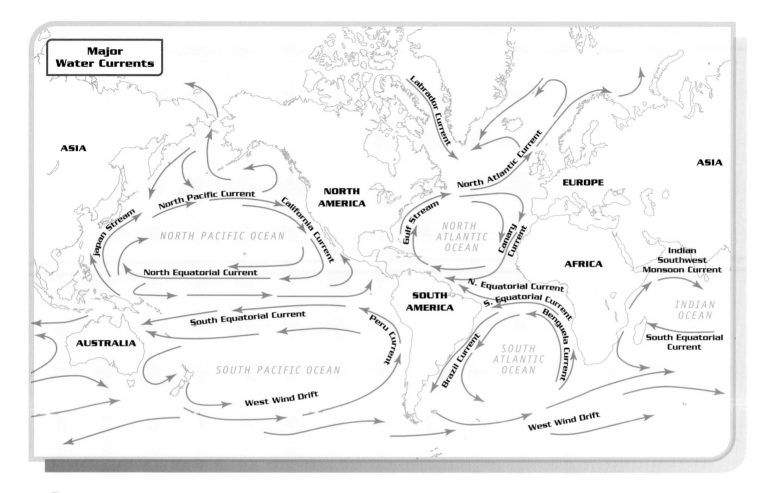

Major Water Currents

The world's oceans are filled with currents: some flow across the globe in a single direction, while others move in a circular pattern.

knot unit of measure of a ship's speed, equal to about 1.15 miles (1.85 km) per hour

salinity saltiness

best-known ocean currents are the Gulf Stream and the California Current. The Gulf Stream, a large warm-water current, flows along the eastern coast of North America and crosses the North Atlantic Ocean to northwestern Europe. The California Current, a cool-water current, moves southward along the western coast of Canada and the United States. Another current, known as the Japan Stream, flows northward through the western Pacific Ocean.

Long ago, mariners learned to adjust the courses of their vessels to take advantage of the extra push provided by ocean currents or at least to avoid sailing against a strong current. Currents are measured in terms of their set—the direction toward which they are flowing—and drift—their speed in **knots.**

A number of factors create currents on the surface of oceans and deep within them. These include wind patterns, variations in the shape of the ocean floor (such as mountains and valleys), the rotation of the Earth, and differences in the temperature and **salinity** of various masses of seawater.

Tides. Tides are vertical movements of the sea. They are caused by the gravitational pull of the Moon and the Sun on water masses, combined with the force of the Earth's rotation on its axis. The horizontal movement of water caused by tides—the rising tide streaming up a beach, for example—is a tidal current.

Every 24-hour period has two high tides when the sea surface rises, or flows, and two low tides when it falls, or ebbs. Tides are most noticeable near coasts, where the rising and falling water can change the visible shoreline dramatically. The difference between the high and low water marks is known as the tidal range. In any body of water, the tidal range and the times that high and low tide occur change from day to day depending on the positions of the Moon and Sun.

Some bodies of water, such as the mostly enclosed Black and Mediterranean Seas, have a small tidal range. In the open ocean the range is larger. The difference between the high and low water marks is greatest in certain river mouths and bays where the shape of the land funnels the tidal current into a confined space. Canada's Bay of Fundy has a spectacular tidal range of up to 50 feet (15 m).

Ship and boat captains need to know about rising and falling tides in harbors, river mouths, and coastal waters to prevent their vessels from running aground at low tide. Many places publish tide tables with daily tidal predictions.

Waves. Waves are regular, repetitive movements of surface water. People who work on water use a variety of terms to describe different kinds of waves. Swells—also known as ground swells—are long, powerful rolling movements that do not break forward into foamy crests. Rips—short, steep waves—occur when two surface currents meet. Chop refers to the small, close waves created by winds on small bodies of water as well as to disturbed surface water produced by the meeting of tidal currents. Surf appears when swells move from deep water into shallower water near land. Surf generally ends in breakers that curl forward and collapse onto the shore.

Mariners use the term *seas* to describe the relationship of waves to vessels. Waves that come from behind a boat and travel in the same direction as the boat are known as following seas. Waves coming toward the boat and moving in the opposite direction to it are head seas. Beam seas refer to waves from the sides. Irregular waves that arrive from two or more directions at once are known as cross seas. A knowledge of waves and seas is very important in navigating a ship. *See also* AIR CURRENT AND WIND; ATLANTIC OCEAN; GULF STREAM; MARITIME HAZARDS; PACIFIC OCEAN; SAILING.

Water Safety

see Ships and Boats, Safety of.

Waterworks

All communities need reliable water supplies—for people to drink and wash with and for industry, agriculture, fire fighting, and hydroelectric power. Throughout history humans have devised various systems to collect water, transport it from place to place, and distribute it.

Early Waterworks. Ancient societies used natural sources of fresh water such as springs and rivers. By about 3000 B.C. they began digging wells to tap underground water supplies. They also collected rainwater in rooftop containers and began storing water in chambers called cisterns, often dug into the ground. At about the same time farmers in Egypt and the Near East began to pump irrigation water into fields.

As cities outgrew their local water supplies, people learned to transport water over distances. The Romans were extremely skillful at building artificial water channels called aqueducts. In the 1600s European cities began using pumps and pipes to distribute water to individual houses.

Modern Waterworks.

Many small towns obtain water from wells. However, wells usually cannot supply enough water to satisfy the needs of a large population. For this reason, cities either take water from lakes or rivers, collect it in artificial lakes called reservoirs, or transport it from other areas. Cincinnati receives water from the Ohio River, and Chicago's water supply comes from Lake Michigan.

There are two basic methods of transporting water: gravity flow and pumping. Gravity allows water to move from a higher to a lower point, such as through aqueducts and out of elevated water towers. Pumps can raise water from wells, force it along an upward slope, or increase the pressure with which it flows through pipes.

Public waterworks usually include a pumping station that draws water into the system from reservoirs, rivers, wells, or other sources. The water may be sent to storage **facilities,** such as water towers. Storing water prevents shortages during dry periods when rainfall and the water levels of wells and rivers may decline.

Water is channeled from the storage facility into water mains, large pipes that run under the streets of cities and towns. Smaller pipes

facilities something built or created to serve a particular function

The Romans were skilled in building aqueducts to carry water to towns and cities. The Pont du Gard aqueduct was built in southern France about 19 B.C. during the reign of Augustus.

branching off from the water mains carry the water to factories, homes, stores, offices, and other buildings. The pumping system supplies enough pressure to cause a steady flow of water when taps are turned on. Raised water towers contribute to water pressure by adding the force of gravity to the flow. Fire hydrants are also connected to public waterworks. They provide access to a high-pressure stream of water that fire-fighting equipment can direct to a nearby blaze.

Water suppliers test and purify water for safety. In dry regions, they follow special procedures to conserve water, such as reducing evaporation in reservoirs. In coastal areas, water systems are designed to prevent seawater from entering the distribution system. *See also* AQUEDUCTS; CANALS; ENERGY; FIRE ENGINES; PIPELINES; RIVERS OF THE WORLD.

Watt, James
Steam engine designer

patent to obtain a legal claim of ownership for an invention

Although James Watt did not invent the steam engine, he improved the early models significantly so that they could be used in transportation and industry. Watt's importance in the development of the engine is reflected in two words: *horsepower,* a term Watt invented, and *watt,* a measure of energy.

Born in 1736 near Greenock, Scotland, Watt developed an interest in tools and machinery in his father's workshop. During the 1750s he started making mathematical instruments such as compasses and scales. His work with steam engines began in the 1760s when he was given an engine to repair. Watt realized that the design was inefficient, and in 1769 he **patented** an improved version of the engine with a separate chamber called a condenser that turned steam back into water.

In 1775 Watt and manufacturer Matthew Boulton began a long partnership to build and sell steam engines. In the following years he continued to improve his designs with features such as speed controls and pressure gauges.

By the time Watt retired from business in 1800, his engines were widely used in mills and canals as well as in many other industries. Income from his many patents had made Watt a wealthy man. He spent his last years continuing to work as an inventor and receiving honors from several nations. He died in 1819. *See also* ENGINES.

Weather

When an unexpected early winter storm buried Denver, Colorado, under 20 inches (51 cm) of snow in October 1997, flights into and out of Denver International Airport were canceled. Three thousand stranded travelers spent an unplanned night in the building. Such incidents serve as a reminder that travel and transportation are often at the mercy of one of the most powerful and uncontrollable forces in the world—the weather.

The effects of weather on travel and transportation range from the inconvenient to the disastrous. Many accidents and tragedies are due to weather. Rain, snow, or ice may make a highway slippery and result in a collision between two cars. A sudden, unexpected wind shift can make it difficult to control an aircraft. Just as families often check the weather forecast before planning a weekend trip, transportation industries rely on highly sophisticated weather monitoring and reporting systems to keep travel problems to a minimum.

Further Information
To learn more about weather, including global weather patterns and the effect of weather on transportation, see the related articles listed at the end of this entry.

maneuver to make a series of changes in course

Weather Conditions

Weather consists of such elements as clouds and fog, precipitation, temperature, winds, and various types of storms. Each of these elements—or a combination of them—can influence travel and transportation.

Clouds and Fog. Clouds form when warm, moist air cools and changes into very tiny droplets of water. A mass of these droplets appears as a cloud. Fog is simply a cloud resting on or near the ground.

Clouds and fog affect transportation chiefly by limiting visibility. Thick clouds and fog form a barrier, making it difficult—and sometimes impossible—for pilots, ship captains, and motorists to see what lies ahead.

Mariners have always had to cope with fog at sea, and devices such as lighthouses, foghorns, and bells have been used to guide ships and help them avoid dangers. Clouds in the atmosphere became a transportation problem only after the beginning of air travel. Until the invention of radar and other electronic navigational tools, pilots needed to be able to see where they were going.

Modern navigational tools allow both aircraft pilots and ship captains to **maneuver** their craft in clouds and fog. Fog remains a problem for motorists, although special lights on cars and trucks may help to some extent. Poor visibility may cause drivers to change travel plans.

Precipitation. When the water droplets in clouds become large enough, they fall, or precipitate. Drops smaller than 0.02 inch (0.5 mm) in diameter come down in the form of drizzle. Larger drops fall as rain. Precipitation may also fall as snow, sleet (slushy, partly frozen ice particles), hail (hard pellets of ice), or freezing rain.

All forms of precipitation can limit visibility. For this reason, many types of vehicles are equipped with windshield wipers to clear rain and snow from the front (and sometimes rear) windows. Precipitation can also make roads dangerously slippery. Rain may cause cars to hydroplane—skid on a thin film of water. Floods resulting from extreme rainfall can wash out roads and bridges.

People who live in regions with cold winter weather must learn to drive on snow. They often take special precautions such as using studded tires or chains to increase traction on snow or ice. In very cold regions, drivers use special heaters to warm up car engines enough to start. In many places, state or local authorities treat snowy or icy roads with salt to speed the melting or with sand to improve traction. They also use plows to move snow from streets and roadways. Sometimes roads are closed because of heavy snowfall or icy conditions.

Freezing rain is an especially serious transportation hazard because it forms a thin, slippery sheet of ice on the ground that is difficult to see. Ice storms of freezing rain can close airports as well as highways. Freezing

Heavy fog limits visibility and can make traveling dangerous. Airplane pilots and ship captains must rely on navigation instruments in foggy conditions.

atmospheric pressure *pressure exerted by the Earth's atmosphere at any given point on the planet's surface*

rain can also prevent aircraft from functioning properly and must be removed with deicing devices.

Wind. Winds are movements of air caused by differences in the **atmospheric pressure** of large air masses. These differences result from variations in temperature at and above the Earth's surface. Winds are one of the principal forces shaping weather on a worldwide, regional, and local scale.

Wind has been both a blessing and a curse to travelers. Winds are the driving force of sailing ships, and countless voyages of exploration and trade could not have taken place without them. Nowadays almost all sailing vessels are pleasure craft, and commercial ships use other sources of power. Yet the wind still plays a role in transportation. Strong winds can put small boats in peril and make travel aboard ships uncomfortable. Abrupt and violent changes in wind sometimes endanger aircraft during takeoff or landing. Sudden storms or shifts in air currents may be the cause of accidents that have occurred in the Bermuda Triangle, an area of the Atlantic Ocean near the southeastern coast of the United States where many planes and ships have disappeared.

Airlines try to plan the routes of long-distance flights to take advantage of tailwinds and avoid headwinds. Tailwinds, which blow in the same direction as the aircraft, increase the plane's speed and allow more efficient use of fuel. Headwinds, which blow against the aircraft, can cause a plane to lose speed and consume a greater amount of fuel.

Motor vehicles are also affected by wind. If a strong, sudden gust strikes the side of a car or truck, it can cause the driver to lose control.

Storms. Of all the weather conditions that affect travel and transportation, the violent atmospheric disturbances called storms pose the greatest hazard to travelers on land, sea, or air. Storms can impair visibility, cause people to lose control of vehicles, and pose other dangers.

Most storms in the United States are the result of weather patterns called extratropical (meaning "outside the tropics") cyclones, which consist of rotating wind systems. Extratropical cyclones affect large areas, usually for several days at a time. Intense disturbances that bring rain, lightning, and thunder to smaller areas for short periods are called thunderstorms.

Tornadoes—whirling, funnel-shaped clouds of water droplets and dust formed by high winds rotating at up to 300 miles per hour (483 km per hour)—have the power to throw cars, trucks, and even houses into the air. Tornadoes that form at sea, usually in the tropics, consist of water droplets only and are called waterspouts. Less violent and dangerous than land tornadoes, they can pose some danger to small ships and boats.

Large tropical storms with wind patterns rotating at speeds of more than 75 miles per hour (121 km per hour) are called tropical cyclones, hurricanes, or typhoons. Such storms are among the most destructive forces in nature. They pose a serious threat to anything in their path, including ships at sea, bridges, highways, and airports.

Meteorology and Weather Forecasting

With all of the problems that weather can cause for transportation, it is little wonder that travelers have always been interested in determining what type of weather lies ahead.

The wisdom of untold generations of travelers, especially sailors, took the form of weather proverbs. These easy-to-remember weather tips, based on long observation and experience, can be quite helpful. For example, the saying "Sharp horns on the Moon threaten high winds" means that if the ends of the crescent Moon are clearly visible, a windy day will follow. This saying reflects the fact that winds are clearing away clouds high in the atmosphere, and those winds will eventually reach the Earth's surface.

Although folk wisdom offers some practical help in forecasting the weather, modern travelers and transportation workers rely on **meteorology** for information. Weather forecasts based on scientific methods appeared during the 1800s. Observers at many different locations recorded data on temperature, wind speed and direction, atmospheric pressure, rainfall, and visibility. Using the telegraph to transmit this information quickly, they were able to create synoptic weather maps—maps showing patterns of pressure, wind, and other meteorological features over a large area at a specific time. Synoptic maps still have a role in weather forecasting, although meteorologists now rely on tools such as radar, weather balloons, and satellites for gathering data and on computers for creating maps and predicting future trends.

The United States established the first systematic weather service in 1871 to issue warnings about storms on the Atlantic and Gulf coasts and the Great Lakes. Today the National Weather Service bases its forecasts on numerical weather prediction (NWP). Using computers, meteorologists create NWP models by assembling huge amounts of data on

Invisible Danger

Aircraft pilots can usually deal with steady winds. But sudden, sharp changes in wind present a danger—a danger that is all the more deadly because it cannot be seen. A change in the wind's speed or direction over a short distance creates a sudden movement of the air called wind shear. A violent downward surge of air that strikes the ground and spreads outward is a microburst wind shear. These forceful atmospheric events have caused a number of plane crashes. During the 1990s commercial airliners in the United States were equipped with instruments designed to help pilots predict and detect wind shear conditions, and many airports have installed special types of radar to detect these dangerous winds.

meteorology scientific study of weather and weather forecasting

A tornado's powerful winds can be devastating to travelers and vehicles caught in its path.

weather observations and applying mathematical formulas to extend past and present trends into the future.

The short-term and long-term weather forecasts of meteorologists are communicated to the public and to transportation industries by the National Weather Service, the Coast Guard, and the National Oceanic and Atmospheric Administration (NOAA). These forecasts make better travel planning possible for individuals and businesses.

The science of meteorology and weather forecasting continues to develop. But it is not—and perhaps never will be—completely accurate. Travelers around the world thus continue to face uncertain, exciting, and sometimes dangerous weather. *See also* ACCIDENTS; AIR CURRENT AND WIND; ATMOSPHERIC PRESSURE; BERMUDA TRIANGLE; GULF STREAM; JET STREAM; LIGHTHOUSES AND LIGHTSHIPS; MARITIME HAZARDS; NAVIGATION; RADAR.

Webb, James
NASA administrator

James Webb (1906–1992) served as administrator of the National Aeronautics and Space Administration (NASA) from 1961 to 1968. He was named to the post just after President John Kennedy announced the project to land an American on the Moon before 1970.

Webb studied law and served in many government posts during his career, experience that later proved invaluable for NASA. He built political support and obtained funds for the enormously expensive space program. Then, in 1967, three astronauts died in a tragic fire during a training exercise for *Apollo 1*. Webb led the investigation of the accident, tried to identify problems, and set the space program back on course. Although he left NASA the following year, the Moon landing took place on schedule in 1969. After retiring from NASA, he served as an adviser to the Smithsonian Institution. *See also* Accidents; Apollo Program; NASA; Space Exploration.

Weightlessness

see Space Travel.

Wells Fargo

For a brief but profitable period in the late 1800s, Wells, Fargo & Company played a major role in transportation in the American West. Using stagecoaches and fast riders, the company built an empire based on banking and express shipping.

Henry Wells, William G. Fargo, and others founded the company in 1852, a few years after the discovery of gold in California. The U.S. mail service had not yet begun delivering parcels, and miners and bankers needed a fast and secure way to send gold dust and nuggets to Eastern banks. Other express companies were operating in the West, but Wells Fargo soon established itself as the leading banking and shipping firm. At first the company sent its parcels from San Francisco to the East Coast by ship. After 1855 it began operating stagecoach lines and buying up competitors. Wells Fargo even owned the Pony Express for a few months. But when telegraph service began, sending messages by horseback seemed hopelessly slow.

By 1866 Wells Fargo controlled most of the stagecoach traffic in the West and was responsible for mail delivery as well as for express parcel

Wells Fargo offices, such as this one in Virginia City, Nevada, handled mail and parcel deliveries and provided stagecoach service in the late 1800s.

service. The company had its own detectives to accompany shipments of gold, silver, and cash. However, the growth of the railroads put the stagecoaches out of business, and in 1913 the U.S. government introduced parcel post, which cut into the parcel-delivery market. Wells, Fargo & Company increasingly focused on banking. Its successor firm is active today in the banking business under the name Wells Fargo. Other security and express businesses have bought or inherited the right to use the Wells Fargo name. *See also* DELIVERY SERVICES; PONY EXPRESS; STAGECOACHES.

Westinghouse, George
American inventor

George Westinghouse (1846–1914) invented the railroad air brake in 1869. Before the invention, brakemen had to run from car to car on a train turning hand brakes after receiving a signal from the engineer. With the air brake, the engineer alone could stop a train. Westinghouse refined his design over a period of years, and modern trains still use the same basic system. Westinghouse is also known for leading the United States to switch from direct current (DC) to alternating current (AC) and for founding the Westinghouse Electric Company, an important manufacturer of electric appliances. *See also* RAILROAD SAFETY.

Wheelchairs

A wheelchair is a seat mounted on four wheels that a person who is unable to walk can use to get around. Wheelchairs range from simple devices propelled by muscle power to sophisticated electric vehicles.

Wheeled chairs date from the 1600s, but the era of the modern wheelchair began in 1932 with the introduction of lightweight folding models. These manual wheelchairs were moved by pushing on the large wheels. Electric wheelchairs became common in the 1960s. In the following years special controls were developed that allowed people who cannot use their arms or hands to operate wheelchair controls with head movements or spoken commands. A few elaborate models feature wheels that can climb stairs and curbs.

mobility ability to move about

The U.S. Census Bureau reported in the 1990s that more than 7 million Americans between ages 17 and 75 had limited **mobility** due to physical disabilities. About half of them used wheelchairs or other devices. Besides providing basic transportation, wheelchairs can be used for a variety of activities, including shopping and sports such as tennis and basketball. A 1990 federal law called the Americans with Disabilities

facilities something built or created to serve a particular function

Act has improved wheelchair access to public **facilities.** New buses, for example, are equipped with lifts that can raise and lower wheelchairs. Such devices are available for private vehicles as well. *See also* BUSES.

Wheels

The wheel, the most important invention in the history of transportation, allowed people to build vehicles that rolled smoothly over the ground. A wheel is a circular disk or frame that rotates around a hub, or center. An axle, which connects the hubs of two wheels, causes the wheels to turn together.

Inventing the Wheel. Experts believe that the wheel was invented in Mesopotamia in the Near East around 3500 B.C. Two-wheeled carts appear in Mesopotamian art from that period, and the remains of wheels have been found in ancient Near Eastern graves. The use of wheeled vehicles gradually spread to surrounding areas, reaching central and northern Europe by about 1000 B.C.

The invention of the wheel may have come from the practice of placing logs as rollers under heavy loads. If some people cut away part of the logs to save weight or increase efficiency, they would have ended up with two wooden disks connected by a bar. That discovery may then have led to the development of separate movable wheels and axles.

The first true wheels were either solid disks of wood or sections of plank clamped together to form a circle. Around 2000 B.C. people in the Near East invented the much lighter spoked wheel, a circular frame linked to the hub by thin bars or rods called spokes. Around this time people also began covering wooden wheels with leather or copper for better resistance to wear and putting copper nails on the rims of wheels for better traction. They also used tar, animal fat, vegetable oil, and leather to lubricate the joints where the wheels and the axles met.

The invention of the wheel allowed people to build vehicles that could roll across the ground. Early carts and wagons opened the way for great advances in transportation.

draft *used for pulling loads*

travois *device consisting of two trailing poles with a net or platform between them to support a load*

Wheeled Vehicles. Among the earliest wheeled vehicles were two-wheeled carts with poles to which **draft** animals could be harnessed. These carts, found in many ancient cultures, may have developed from the **travois.** The first four-wheeled wagons appeared around 2500 B.C., and within a few hundred years such vehicles were common in the Near East and had begun to appear in parts of Europe as well. By about 700 B.C. improvements in ironworking technology led to the development of protective iron covers, or tires, fitted onto wooden wheels. These metal tires gave wheels a much longer life.

The wheel did not revolutionize transportation by itself. Changes in the design of animal harnesses, axles, and steering mechanisms over the centuries helped increase the effectiveness of wheels. Changes in wheel design made wheels stronger and more efficient. Improvements in road-building techniques made road surfaces more suitable for wheeled vehicles.

Wheels are an essential part of almost all forms of modern transportation, from cars and trucks to airplanes and railroads. Moreover, devices based on the principle of the wheel, such as gears and pulleys, are a vital element in engines as well as many machines used in modern societies. *See also* AIRCRAFT, PARTS OF; AUTOMOBILES, PARTS OF; BICYCLES; CARTS, CARRIAGES, AND WAGONS; CHARIOTS; ELEVATORS AND ESCALATORS; GYROSCOPE; RAILWAY TRAINS, PARTS OF; ROADS; TIRES; WHEELCHAIRS.

Wind

see *Air Current and Wind; Weather.*

World War I Planes

see *Aviation, History of.*

World War II Planes

see *Aviation, History of.*

Wright, Orville and Wilbur
Pioneers of flight

Orville and Wilbur Wright, self-taught engineers, built the first successful powered heavier-than-air plane. Its 12-second flight in 1903 marked the beginning of the age of aviation.

Bikes and Kites. Wilbur (born in 1867) and Orville (born in 1871) were the sons of Milton and Susan Wright. Their father encouraged them to think independently and to investigate subjects that interested them. Although neither Wilbur nor Orville went to college, they became very skillful in researching technical topics and setting up practical experiments to test their ideas.

During the 1890s the brothers ran a print shop in their hometown of Dayton, Ohio. Their machines earned them a reputation for good workmanship. Later they opened a store where they made, repaired, and sold bicycles.

At the time, inventors around the world were trying to build flying machines. Orville and Wilbur Wright were among those fascinated by the idea of flight. In 1896 glider pioneer Otto Lilienthal died in a crash, an event that prompted the Wright brothers to look seriously into the problems of flight. After studying **aeronautics** and conducting tests in their own wind tunnel, they came to the following conclusion: to control a winged aircraft the pilot needed to be able to warp, or bend, the ends of the wings slightly. The brothers built kites to test their theory and then constructed a glider.

aeronautics the science of flight

From Gliders to Powered Flight. The Wrights decided to carry out their glider experiments at Kitty Hawk, North Carolina, a place that offered open stretches of soft sand and steady breezes. They

Orville and Wilbur Wright's pioneer airplanes and successful test flights made the idea of a flying machine a reality.

built and tested a second glider that incorporated their idea of wing warping and then created a wind tunnel to determine the best possible shape for wing design. After testing more than 100 models of wings, the brothers constructed their third glider. It performed well in hundreds of flights.

The next step was powered, controlled flight. The Wrights designed and built an aircraft with a small gasoline engine that was connected to propellers by a bicycle chain. It was a biplane with two wings, one above the other. Orville made the first successful flight in this machine on December 17, 1903, covering a distance of 120 feet (37 m) in 12 seconds. He had to lie on his stomach facing forward across the lower wing. That craft made a total of four flights that day but never flew again. Today it is displayed at the Smithsonian Institution's National Air and Space Museum in Washington, D.C.

Orville and Wilbur Wright sought little publicity until they were satisfied with their achievement. They returned to Dayton and, over the next two years, developed two more aircraft. Once the planes could stay aloft for more than half an hour and could perform **maneuvers** such as circles, the Wrights sought a **patent** for their invention.

maneuver *series of changes in course*
patent *legal ownership of an invention*

The Business of Flight.

The Wrights' fame did not begin to grow until 1908, when they signed a contract to provide the U.S. Army with military aircraft. Later the brothers carried out flight demonstrations before astonished crowds in the United States and Europe.

Meanwhile the Wrights were involved in a patent dispute with inventor Glenn Curtiss, who flew his own airplane in 1908. Lawsuits and arguments centered on who really invented control devices for the airplane. In the end, the Wrights were given credit for using wing warping.

In 1909 the brothers established companies in both Germany and New York to manufacture airplanes, but they never reaped great profit from their invention. Wilbur died in 1912. Orville continued to work as an aeronautics designer and was a member of the National Advisory Committee for Aeronautics from 1920 until his death in 1948. His contributions helped powered flight develop from a technical accomplishment into an industry that changed the way the world traveled. *See also* Aviation, History of; Curtiss, Glenn; Gliders.

Yachts

A yacht is a privately owned boat or ship. The word *yacht* comes from the Dutch *jachten,* meaning "to hurry" or "to hunt," and the German *jachtschiff,* meaning "hunting ship" or "chasing ship." Early yachts were used by pirates to hunt ships and by other sailors looking for the pirates.

A yacht may be powered by sails, engines, or a combination of the two. Available in a wide variety of designs, most yachts can be classified as either racing yachts or pleasure yachts. Racing models, built for speed rather than comfort, are typically smaller and lighter than pleasure yachts. Yachts designed for entertaining may be hundreds of feet long and have many cabins and decks, as well as full kitchens and bathrooms.

Yacht racing became popular in Holland during the 1600s, and King Charles II of England brought the sport home with him in 1660. One of

Yachts are powered by sails, engines, or a combination of the two. Here, a 142-foot (43-m) yacht motors along a river in the Netherlands.

the first yacht clubs was founded in Ireland in 1720. Yacht clubs appeared in the United States a century later.

Many yachting competitions occur around the world each year. Perhaps the most famous is the America's Cup, first held in 1851 with challenges every few years. Yacht races have also been included in the Olympic Games since 1900. *See also* SAILBOATS AND SAILING SHIPS; SHIPS AND BOATS, TYPES OF.

Yeager, Charles
American pilot

supersonic faster than the speed of sound

American pilot Charles "Chuck" Yeager was the first person to fly faster than the speed of sound—about 660 miles per hour (1,062 km per hour) at an altitude of 37,000 feet (11,278 m). Born in 1923, Yeager served as a fighter pilot in World War II, flying 64 missions and shooting down 13 German planes. Later he became a flight instructor and military test pilot of experimental aircraft. In 1947 Yeager, then a U.S. Air Force captain, was chosen to fly the X-1, a rocket-driven plane built to reach **supersonic** speeds. On October 14, 1947, he took the plane to 43,000 feet (13,106 m), reaching a speed of 700 miles per hour (1,126 km per hour) and breaking the sound barrier. In 1953 he set a world record by flying the X-1A rocket plane at 1,612 miles per hour (2,594 km per hour). Yeager retired from the Air Force with the rank of brigadier general in 1975. *See also* AVIATION, HISTORY OF; SUPERSONIC FLIGHT.

Zeppelins

see Airships.

Time Line

ca. 5000	People in northern Europe use dogs and reindeer to pull sleds Minoans on the island of Crete build seagoing boats
ca. 4000–3000	Egyptians develop sailing ships to use on the Nile River
ca. 3500	Wheel is invented and used in Mesopotamia Oxen, donkeys, and elephants are used to carry and pull loads in Egypt and the Middle East
ca. 3000	Sumerians develop a two-wheeled cart
ca. 3000–2000	Central Asians tame the horse
ca. 2500	Snow skiing begins in Russia and Sweden
ca. 2300	Canals are built in Egypt
ca. 2000	Egyptians develop postal system
ca. 1700	Horses are harnessed to pull two-wheeled vehicles in ancient Mesopotamia
ca. 850	Stone bridge is built in Turkey
680	Olympic Games in ancient Greece include chariot races
ca. 500	Romans build bridges throughout their empire Greeks construct aqueducts to carry water to their cities
483	Athens builds a navy
331	Alexander the Great founds the largest port of the ancient world at Alexandria in Egypt
312	Romans begin building the Appian Way
ca. 300	Aqueducts constructed throughout the Roman Empire
ca. 283–246	Pharos Lighthouse built in Alexandria
36	First tunnel designed for transportation built by Romans

A.D.

ca. 100	Chinese invent a harness that allows horses to pull loads
ca. 150	Ptolemy creates maps of the world
ca. 200	Roman postal network begins carrying private mail
ca. 800–1050	Viking ships sail along northern European coasts
ca. 984	Chinese build locks on canals
1044	Gunpowder is used for rockets in China
1095–1270	Europeans launch the Crusades, a series of military expeditions to the Middle East to recapture the Holy Land from the Muslims

ca. 1100s	Chinese and Mediterranean navigators use magnetic compasses
1270s	Marco Polo travels to China
1480–1483	Leonardo da Vinci conducts studies of flight and sketches a helicopter-like craft
1488	Bartolomeu Dias sails around the Cape of Good Hope on the tip of Africa
1492–1493	Christopher Columbus sails across the Atlantic Ocean and discovers the "New World"
ca. 1500s	Europeans cross the Atlantic Ocean and explore North America in large sailing ships
1519	Hernán Cortés reaches Tenochtitlán, the capital of the Aztec empire
1519–1522	Ferdinand Magellan leads the first circumnavigation of the globe
1520s	Slave trade begins
1530–1533	Francisco Pizarro explores the west coast of South America
1577–1580	Sir Francis Drake leads the second global circumnavigation
1588	Spanish Armada is defeated by England
1600s	Coaches appear on roads in England
1603–1615	Samuel de Champlain explores the St. Lawrence River and establishes the colony of New France
1609	Galileo Galilei uses a telescope for astronomical observation
1620	Cornelius van Drebbel builds the first submarine
ca. 1670	Stagecoach service begins between London and Scotland
1690	Lloyd's of London Insurance Company is founded
1691	Thomas Neale organizes a postal service in the American colonies
1692	Languedoc Canal of France links the Atlantic Ocean and the Mediterranean Sea
1712	Thomas Newcomen builds a successful steam engine
1716	First lighthouse in North America begins operation in Boston Harbor
1750s	Conestoga wagons haul freight westward for pioneers
1760s	British government publishes astronomical tables for navigation
1769	James Watt redesigns the steam engine
1775	U.S. Navy is established David Bushnell builds a military submarine
1779	Cast-iron bridge spanning the Severn River in England opens
1783	James Watt sets "horsepower" measuring standard Montgolfier brothers launch several hot-air balloons
1789	U.S. Congress approves the collection of customs duties U.S. Post Office Department is established
1795	U.S. government builds an engineered road
1798	Richard Trevithick develops a steam engine to drive carriages
early 1800s	Concord Coach is produced in New Hampshire
1802	First tugboat is built
1804–1806	Meriwether Lewis and William Clark lead an expedition of discovery across the Louisiana Territory

1807	Robert Fulton's steamboat *Clermont* begins commercial service Slave trade is abolished
1811	Construction on the Cumberland Road begins
1814	George Stephenson builds the first steam locomotive
1819	The steamboat *Savannah* makes a transatlantic journey
1825	Erie Canal is completed, linking the Hudson River to the Great Lakes Stockton and Darlington Railway opens in England
1827	Baltimore and Ohio Railroad is founded
1833	First American rail tunnel is built
1837	Samuel F. B. Morse invents the telegraph
1840	Cunard Line launches its first steamship
1845	Thomas Cook opens the first travel agency Pneumatic tire is invented
1848	Gold is discovered in California
1852	Henri Giffard builds and pilots the first powered airship First horse-drawn streetcar appears in New York City
1853	Elisha Otis introduces an automatic safety device for the elevator George Cayley designs the first successful glider plane
1859–1860	Jean-Joseph-Etienne Lenoir patents an internal combustion engine
1860s	American "prairie schooner" wagons take settlers west
1860–1861	Pony Express mail service begins
1861	U.S. transcontinental telegraph is completed
1863	First underground railway (subway) opens in London
ca. 1865	Ambulance carriage service begins in Cincinnati, Ohio
1865–1866	Workers lay a telegraph cable across the Atlantic Ocean
1869	George Westinghouse invents the railroad air brake Suez Canal opens Transcontinental Railroad is completed in the United States
ca. 1870	"High-wheeler" bicycle is developed
1871	Elevated trains begin operation in New York City
1873	Andrew Hallidie develops a system to run cable cars in San Francisco
1876	Alexander Graham Bell invents the telephone
1880	First electric elevator is built in Germany
1883	Standard time zones system is adopted in the United States
1884	Charles Parsons develops the steam turbine
1885	Karl Benz and Gottlieb Daimler both develop gasoline-powered engines
1887	U.S. Interstate Commerce Commission is created
1889	Gottlieb Daimler and Wilhelm Maybach produce a motor vehicle with a gasoline engine and found an auto company

1890s	Rudolf Diesel develops the diesel engine
1891	Escalator is invented
1892–1893	Frank and Charles Duryea build the first gasoline-powered automobiles in the United States
1894	Major railway strikes take place in the United States
1895	Guglielmo Marconi invents the radio
1896	Gottlieb Daimler produces the first truck
1897	Subway service begins in Boston
1898	John Holland builds a practical submarine
	USS *Maine* sinks off Cuba
1900	Count Ferdinand von Zeppelin launches an airship
	Paris subway opens
1901	First American motorcycle with a gasoline engine is manufactured
1902	American Automobile Association (AAA) is founded
	Cadillac Automobile Company is created by Henry M. Leland
1903	Orville and Wilbur Wright make the first successful flight in a heavier-than-air plane at Kitty Hawk, North Carolina, on December 17
	Henry Ford founds the Ford Motor Company in Detroit
1904	New York City subway opens
1905	Enrico Forlanini invents the hydrofoil
1906	First modern battleship is launched
1907	United Parcel Service (UPS) is founded in Seattle, Washington
1908	Henry Ford introduces the first Model T Ford
	Dogsled races begin in Alaska
1909	Louis Blériot flies across the English Channel between France and England
	General Motors buys the Cadillac Automobile Company
1911–1912	Glenn Curtiss designs the first amphibian and flying boat
1911	Chevrolet Motor Car Company is established in Detroit by William Durant and Louis Chevrolet
1912	*Titanic* sinks during its first voyage
1913	Grand Central Terminal in New York City opens
	Henry Ford introduces the moving assembly line method of building cars
1914	Traffic lights are introduced
	Greyhound Corporation is founded in Minnesota
1915	*Lusitania* sinks
	U.S. Coast Guard is formed
1916	General Motors acquires Chevrolet
	U.S. Congress passes legislation to build and maintain the nation's highways
	Trans-Siberian Railroad is completed within Russian borders
1918	U.S. Post Office launches airmail service
1919	Scheduled airline passenger service is introduced
1920	Panama Canal begins full operation

1921 First drive-in restaurant opens

1922 First shopping center in the United States opens

1923 Hermann Oberth publishes his work on the theory of space flight

1925 United States introduces uniform road signs and adopts a route-numbering system
A. Philip Randolph forms the Brotherhood of Sleeping Car Porters

1926 Robert Goddard designs the first successful liquid-fuel rocket
Air Commerce Act is passed by Congress to regulate air transportation

1927 Charles Lindbergh flies nonstop across the Atlantic Ocean in 33.5 hours
Holland Tunnel, the first underwater road tunnel, opens, connecting New York City and New Jersey

1930 Bathysphere is invented

1932 Amelia Earhart completes the first solo flight by a woman across the Atlantic Ocean

1933 Wiley Post flies around the world and sets a speed record
First drive-in movie theater opens

1937 *Hindenburg,* an airship fueled by hydrogen, explodes just before landing in New Jersey

1939 Igor Sikorsky builds and flies the first helicopter

1940 Civil Aeronautics Board is created to regulate airlines and ensure safe operating procedures

1943 Jacques-Yves Cousteau develops a scuba system for underwater diving

1945 International Air Transport Association is formed
Enola Gay drops the first atomic bomb on Hiroshima, Japan, on August 6

1947 Pilot Charles Yeager breaks the sound barrier and achieves supersonic flight
Thor Heyerdahl sails from Peru to eastern Polynesia in a raft
U.S. Department of the Air Force is created

1950 First automatic elevators are installed

1952 Passenger service in jet planes begins with the British de Havilland Comet

1954 First nuclear-powered submarine, *Nautilus,* is launched

1956 Federal Aid Highway Act paves the way for the Interstate Highway System in the United States
Andrea Doria and the *Stockholm* collide off the coast of Nantucket
First enclosed mall opens in Minnesota

1957 Soviets launch *Sputnik 1,* the first satellite to orbit the Earth, on October 4

1958 FAA (Federal Aviation Administration) is created
First U.S. artificial satellite, *Explorer 1,* is launched on January 31
NASA is formed

1959 St. Lawrence Seaway opens
First air-cushion vehicle is launched

1960s Airlines begin using computer reservation systems

1960 NASA launches *Tiros 1,* the world's first weather satellite

1961 Soviets launch *Vostok 1* with Yuri Gagarin aboard on April 12; he becomes the first human in space
Alan Shepard becomes the first American to travel in space on May 5

1962 John Glenn orbits the Earth on February 20

1963   Pan American Highway opens

1964–1965   Intelsat communications system is established

1965   Alexei Leonov becomes the first person to walk in space on March 18
Ralph Nader publishes *Unsafe at Any Speed,* a scathing criticism of the auto industry

1966   U.S. Department of Transportation is created

1967   National Transportation Safety Board is established

1968   *Apollo 8,* a piloted spacecraft, orbits the Moon on December 21

1969   Neil Armstrong and Edwin "Buzz" Aldrin, Jr. land on Moon on July 20 during the *Apollo 11* mission

1970   U.S. government passes the Clean Air Act
Amtrak is established

1971   Soviet Union launches *Salyut 1,* the world's first space station, on April 19

1973   U.S. space station, *Skylab,* is launched on May 14
Conrail is created
Federal Express is formed

1974   BART (Bay Area Rapid Transit) network opens in San Francisco

1975   Soviet and U.S. spacecraft, *Soyuz 19* and *Apollo 18,* dock in space on July 15
European Space Agency is established

1976   Supersonic jet, *Concorde,* begins service

1977   NASA launches Voyager probes to explore the outer planets of the solar system
Trans-Alaska Pipeline is completed

1978   Airline Deregulation Act is passed

1981   First orbital flight of *Columbia,* a U.S. space shuttle
TGV high-speed train begins service in France

1983   Sally Ride, the first American woman in space, joins the crew of space shuttle *Challenger*

1986   U.S. space shuttle *Challenger* explodes during its launch on January 28
Soviet space station *Mir* is launched

1990   Hubble Space Telescope is launched aboard the space shuttle *Discovery*

1994   Channel Tunnel is completed, connecting England and France

1997   *Mars Pathfinder* sends a rover vehicle to collect soil samples on Mars

1998   First section of the *International Space Station* is launched into orbit
Chrysler merges with the Daimler-Benz Company
CSX and Norfolk Southern/railroads acquire Conrail
John Glenn returns to space at age 77 on the space shuttle *Discovery*

1999   *Mars Polar Lander* searches for water at Mars's southern pole
Amtrak introduces high-speed Acela train service between Boston and Washington, D.C.
Bertrand Piccard and Brian Jones become the first balloonists to travel nonstop around the world
Eileen M. Collins becomes the first woman to command a space shuttle flight

Suggested Readings

General

Bruno, Leonard C. *On the Move: A Chronology of Advances in Transportation.* Detroit: Gale Research, 1993.

Butterfield, Moira. *Wheels, Wings, and Moving Things.* Parsippany, N.J.: Silver Burdett Press, 1999.

Cayton, Mary Kupiec, Elliott J. Gorn, and Peter W. Williams, eds. *Encyclopedia of American Social History.* 3 vols. New York: Charles Scribner's Sons, 1993.

*Graham, Ian. *Cars, Planes, Ships, and Trains.* New York: Facts on File, 1995.

Hawkes, Nigel. *Vehicles.* New York: Macmillan, 1991.

*————. *Transportation on Land and Sea.* New York: Twenty-First Century Press, 1994.

Krieger, Michael. *Where Rails Meet the Sea.* New York: Metro Books, 1998.

Lay, M. G. *Ways of the World: A History of the World's Roads and of the Vehicles That Used Them.* New Brunswick, N.J.: Rutgers University Press, 1992.

Richter, William L. *The ABC-CLIO Companion to Transportation in America.* Santa Barbara, Calif.: ABC-CLIO, 1995.

Williams, Brian. *The History of Transportation.* New York: Thomson Learning, 1996.

Wood, Michael. *Ancient Transportation: From Camels to Canals.* Minn.: Lerner Publications, 1999.

Aviation

Bilstein, Roger E. *Flight in America: From the Wrights to the Astronauts.* Baltimore: Johns Hopkins Universtiy Press, 1994.

Douglas, Deborah. *United States Women in Aviation, 1941–1985.* Washington, D.C.: Smithsonian Institution, 1991.

Ethell, Jeffrey L. *Frontiers of Flight.* Washington, D.C.: Smithsonian Books, 1992.

Heppenheimer, T. A. *Turbulent Skies: The History of Commercial Aviation.* New York: John Wiley, 1995.

Howard, Fred. *Wilbur and Orville: A Biography of the Wright Brothers.* Mineola, N.Y.: Dover Publications, 1998.

Lopez, Donald S. *Aviation: A Smithsonian Guide.* New York: Macmillan, 1995.

Serling, Robert J. *The Epic of Flight.* Alexandria, Va.: Time-Life Books, 1982.

Spenser, Jay P. *Whirlybirds: A History of the U.S. Helicopter Pioneers.* Seattle, Wash.: University of Washington, 1998

Williams, George. *The Airline Industry and the Impact of Deregulation.* Brookfield, Vt.: Ashgate, 1993.

Maritime

Bourne, Russell. *Floating West: The Erie and Other American Canals.* New York: Norton, 1992.

Culver, Henry B. *The Book of Old Ships: From Egyptian Galleys to Clipper Ships.* New York: Dover, 1992.

Edmunds, Arthur. *Designing Power and Sail.* Enola, Pa.: Bristol Fashion Publications, 1998.

Gardiner, Robert, ed. *The Earliest Ships: The Evolution of Boats into Ships.* London: Conway Maritime Press, 1996.

*Graham, Ian. *Boats, Ships, Submarines, and Other Floating Machines.* New York: Kingfisher Books, 1993.

Greenhill, Basil. *The Archaeology of Boats and Ships: An Introduction.* Annapolis, Md.: Naval Institute Press, 1996.

Jones, Dilwyn. *Boats.* Austin, Tex.: University of Texas Press, 1995.

Kemp, Peter. *The Oxford Companion to Ships and the Sea.* Oxford: Oxford University Press, 1988.

Paine, Lincoln P. *Ships of the World: An Historical Encyclopedia.* Boston: Houghton Mifflin, 1992.

Books marked with an asterisk (*) are suitable for a young audience.

Pedraja, René de la. *A Historical Dictionary of the U.S. Merchant Marine and Shipping Industry.* Westport, Conn.: Greenwood, 1994.

Shaw, Ronald E. *Canals for a Nation: The Canal Era in the United States, 1790–1860.* Lexington, Ky.: University Press of Kentucky, 1990.

Woodman, Richard. *The History of the Ship: The Comprehensive Story of Seafaring from the Earliest Times to the Present Day.* New York: Lyons Press, 1997.

Motor Vehicles

Belasco, Warren James. *Americans on the Road: From Autocamp to Motel, 1910–1945.* Baltimore: Johns Hopkins University Press, 1997.

Coffey, Frank, and Joseph Layden. *America on Wheels: The First 100 Years.* Los Angeles: General Publishing Group, 1996.

Flink, James J. *The Automobile Age.* Cambridge, Mass.: MIT Press, 1988.

Flower, Raymond. *100 Years on the Road: A Social History of the Car.* New York: McGraw-Hill, 1981.

Ierley, Merritt. *Traveling the National Road: Across the Centuries on America's First Highway.* Woodstock, N.Y.: Overlook Press, 1990.

Mandell, Susan Meikle, et al. *A Historical Survey of Transit Buses in the United States.* Warrendale, Pa.: Society of Automotive Engineers, 1990.

McShane, Clay. *Down the Asphalt Path: The Automobile and the American City.* New York: Columbia Press, 1994.

Rothe, J. Peter. *The Trucker's World: Risk, Safety, and Mobility.* New Brunswick, N.J.: Transaction Publishers, 1991.

Wakefield, Ernest Henry. *History of the Electric Automobile: Hybrid Electric Vehicles.* Warrendale, Pa.: Society of Automotive Engineers, 1998.

Railroads

Comstock, Henry B. *The Iron Horse: An Illustrated History of Steam Locomotives.* New York: Greenberg Publications, 1993.

DeBoer, David J. *Piggyback and Containers: A History of Rail Intermodal on America's Steel Highway.* San Marino, Calif.: Golden West Books, 1992.

Drury, George H. *Guide to North American Steam Locomotives.* Milwaukee: Kalmbach, 1993.

Folsom, Burton. *The Myth of the Robber Barons.* Herndon, Va.: Young America's Foundation, 1991.

Goddard, Stephen B. *Getting There: The Epic Struggle Between Road and Rail in the American Century.* Chicago: University of Chicago Press, 1996.

Gordon, Sarah H. *Passage to Union: How the Railroads Transformed American Life, 1829–1929.* Chicago: Ivan R. Dee, 1996.

Martin, Albro. *Railroads Triumphant: The Growth, Rejection, and Rebirth of a Vital American Force.* New York: Oxford University Press, 1992.

Riley, C. J. *The Encyclopedia of Trains and Locomotives.* New York: Metro Books, 1995.

Space

Barbree, Jay. *A Journey Through Time: Exploring the Universe with the Hubble Space Telescope.* New York: Penguin Studio, 1995.

Bilstein, Roger E. *Orders of Magnitude: A History of the NACA and NASA, 1915–1990.* Washington, D.C.: National Aeronautics and Space Administration Office of Management, Scientific and Technical Information Division, 1989.

Bond, Peter. *Heroes in Space: From Gagarin to Challenger.* New York: Basil Blackwell, Inc., 1989.

Burrows, William E. *Exploring Space: Voyages in the Solar System and Beyond.* New York: Random House, 1990.

Chaikin, Andrew. *A Man on the Moon: The Voyages of the Apollo Astronauts.* New York: Viking, 1994.

Clark, Philip. *The Soviet Manned Space Program.* New York: Orion Books, 1988.

Davies, J. K. *Space Exploration.* New York: Chambers, 1992.

Heppenheimer, T. A. *Countdown: A History of Space Flight.* New York: John Wiley, 1997.

*Kennedy, Gregory P. *Apollo to the Moon.* New York: Chelsea House, 1992.

*———. *First Men in Space.* New York: Chelsea House, 1991.

Murray, Bruce. *Journey into Space: The First Three Decades of Space Exploration.* New York: W. W. Norton & Company, Inc., 1989.

Neal, Valerie, Cathleen S. Lewis, and Frank H. Winter. *Spaceflight: A Smithsonian Guide.* New York: Macmillan, 1995.

Raeburn, Paul. *Mars: Uncovering the Secrets of the Red Planet.* Washington, D.C.: National Geographic Society, 1998.

Shepard, Alan B., and Donald K. Slayton. *Moon Shot: The Inside Story of America's Race to the Moon.* Atlanta, Ga.: Turner Publications, 1992.

*Vogt, Gregory. *The Solar System: Facts and Exploration.* New York: Twenty-First Century Books, 1995.

Winter, Frank H. *Rockets into Space.* Cambridge, Mass.: Harvard University Press, 1990.

On-Line Resources

Airports Council International
http://www.airports.org

Air Transport Association
http://www.air-transport.org

American Automobile Association
http://www.aaa.com

American Automobile Manufacturers Association
http://www.aama.com

American Public Transit Association
http://www.apta.com

American Society of Travel Agents
http://www.astanet.com

Amtrak
http://www.amtrak.com

Bureau of Transportation Statistics
http://www.bts.gov

Discoverers Web
http://www.win.tue.nl/cs/fm/engels/ discovery/

Environmental Protection Agency
http://www.epa.gov

Federal Aviation Administration
http://www.faa.gov

Federal Highway Administration
http://www.fhwa.dot.gov

Federal Railroad Administration
http://www.fra.dot.gov

Federal Trade Commission
http://www.ftc.gov

Federal Transit Administration
http://www.fts.dot.gov

International Air Transport Association
http://www.iata.org

Lewis and Clark
http://www.pbs.org/lewisandclark

National Aeronautics and Space Administration
http://www.nasa.gov

National Highway Traffic Safety Administration
http://www.nhtsa.dot.gov

National Transportation Safety Board
http://www.ntsb.gov

Panama Canal Commission
http://www.pancanal.com

Saint Lawrence Seaway Development Corporation
http://www.dot.gov/slsdc/

Surface Transportation Board
http://www.stb.dot.gov

Transportation History, Smithsonian Institution
http://www.si.edu/resource/faq/nmah/transportation.html

Transport Workers Union of America
http://www.twu.com

Travel Industry Association of America
http://www.tia.org

U.S. Coast Guard
http://www.uscg.mil/

U.S. Customs Service
http://www.customs.treas.gov

U.S. Department of Commerce
http://www.doc.gov

U.S. Department of Transportation
http://www.dot.gov

U.S. International Trade Commission
http://www.usitc.gov

U.S. Maritime Administration
http://www.marad.dot.gov

U.S. Postal Service
http://www.usps.gov

World Tourism Organization
http://www.world-tourism.org

Glossary

aerodynamic relating to the motion of air and the effects of such motion on planes and other objects

aerodynamics branch of science that deals with the motion of air and the effects of such motion on planes and other objects

aeronautical relating to the science of flight

aeronautics the science of flight

aileron movable section on aircraft wing, used to turn the plane

airship large aircraft filled with lighter-than-air gas that keeps it aloft; also known as a blimp

allegorical relating to a literary device in which characters represent an idea or a religious or moral principle

amphibious able to move on land and through water

anchorage area in which vessels can ride at anchor

aqueduct artificial channel for carrying water

archaeologist scientist who studies past human cultures, usually by digging up ruins

armada fleet of warships

artifact ornament, tool, weapon, or other object made by humans

artillery heavy weapons or guns that fire missiles and other projectiles

ascension rising, flight

assembly line production system in which tasks are performed in sequence by an arrangement of workers and equipment

astrolabe navigational instrument used since ancient times to determine distance north or south of the equator

astronomical having to do with the study of the stars, planets, and so on

atmospheric pressure pressure exerted by the Earth's atmosphere at any given point on the planet's surface

avionics electronics system used in airplanes, missiles, and rockets

bank to tilt

boom long pole extending from the mast of a boat

brig small, fast-sailing ship with two masts and square sails

buoy floating marker in the water

buoyancy force that exerts an upward push on an object

caravel small ship with three masts and both square and triangular sails

carburetor device that supplies an explosive mixture of fuel and air to an engine

cardinal directions north, south, east, and west

cartography science of mapmaking

celestial having to do with the sky or heavens

chassis main body or frame of a vehicle

circumnavigate to travel around

circumnavigation journey around the world

civilian nonmilitary

Cold War period of tense relations between the United States and the Soviet Union following World War II

combustion process of burning

component element or part that makes up a whole

constellation recognizable pattern of stars

containerization method of shipping cargo in boxlike containers that can be transferred from one type of transportation to another

conveyor mechanical device for moving articles on a belt or chain from one place to another

convoy group of ships, aircraft, or land vehicles that travel together for security and convenience

cosmonaut Russian term for a person who travels into space; literally, "traveler to the universe"

Crusades series of wars in the Middle Ages in which European Christians attempted to win the Holy Land from the Muslims

customs tax on imported goods

deregulation process of removing restrictions and regulations

dirigible large aircraft filled with a lighter-than-air gas that keeps it aloft; similar to a blimp but with a rigid frame

doldrums areas of calm or light winds in ocean regions near the equator

domestic relating to activities or products made within a country

draft used for pulling loads

drag slowing effect of an opposing force, such as friction, on a vehicle

embargo government order prohibiting trade with another country

emissions substances discharged into the air

facilities something built or created to serve a particular function

friction force that produces a resistance to motion

frigate small, agile warship with three masts and square sails

guided missile missile, or rocket, steered by radio signals and electronic codes

gyroscope spinning mechanism that maintains its position even when the framework supporting it is tilted

hydraulic operated by or using water or other liquids in motion

imperial relating to an empire or emperor

internal combustion engine engine powered by burning a mixture of fuel and air inside narrow chambers called cylinders

jet lag fatigue and irritability after a long flight through several time zones

keel wood or metal structure that runs lengthwise along the bottom of a boat and helps strengthen it

keelboat narrow riverboat used to transport freight

knot unit of measure of a ship's speed, equal to about 1.15 miles (1.85 km) per hour

latitude distance north or south of the equator

lift force that pushes an aircraft (or other body) up and keeps it airborne

longitude distance east or west of the prime meridian, an imaginary line on the Earth's surface that runs through Greenwich, England

lunar referring to the Moon

maneuver (v) to make a series of changes in course; (n) series of changes in course

maritime related to the sea or shipping

mass transit system of public transportation in an urban area

merchant marine vessels engaged in commerce; officers and crews of such vessels

meteorological having to do with weather

meteorology scientific study of weather and weather forecasting

metropolitan relating to a large city and the surrounding suburbs

NASA National Aeronautics and Space Administration, the U.S. space agency

nautical relating to ships and sailors

navigable deep or wide enough for boats or ships to pass through

oceanography scientific study of the ocean and underwater life

orbiter piloted section of a space shuttle that goes into space

packet small, fast ship used during the 1800s to carry mail, cargo, and passengers

patent (v) to obtain a legal claim of ownership for an invention; (n) legal ownership of an invention

payload object placed in space by a launch vehicle; any type of cargo carried aboard a spacecraft

phenomenon an observable fact or occurrence

pilgrimage journey to a sacred place

piston mechanical part moved back and forth by fluid pressure inside a chamber

pneumatic filled with or operated by compressed air

pollutant something that contaminates the environment

probe uncrewed spacecraft sent out to explore and collect information in space

propulsion process of driving or propelling

prototype first working example of a new design

reconnaissance act of searching, inspecting, and observing for the purpose of gaining information

rigging network of lines or ropes that raises, lowers, and positions a ship's sails

running board narrow footboard on the side of an automobile

salinity saltiness

salvage saving or recovering property lost underwater

schooner fast, easy-to-maneuver sailing ship with two or more masts and triangular sails

scuba equipment that allows a diver to carry oxygen underwater; letters stand for "self-contained underwater breathing apparatus"

sediment material that settles to the bottom of a liquid

sensor device that reacts to changes in light, heat, motion, and so on

sextant instrument used by navigators since the 1750s to determine distance north or south of the equator

simulated imitating special conditions for test purposes

sonar short for sound navigation and ranging; system that uses sound waves to locate underwater objects

sound barrier sudden increase in air resistance that occurs when an aircraft approaches the speed of sound

Soviet Union nation that existed from 1922 to 1991, made up of Russia and 14 other republics in eastern Europe and northern Asia

submersible small submarine used for research or as a base for divers

suborbital refers to flight into space that does not go into orbit

supersonic faster than the speed of sound

suspension system of springs and other parts that supports the body of a vehicle on the axles

tariff system of taxes on imported or exported goods

tempered treated to make harder or stronger

territorial waters inland and coastal waters under the authority of a state or nation

torque turning force

trade winds winds that blow from east to west in the tropics

transatlantic relating to crossing the Atlantic Ocean

transcontinental extending across a continent

transoceanic extending across an ocean

tributary stream or river that flows into a larger stream or river

turbulence irregular movement of air, especially up and down

vacuum empty space with low air pressure

Photo Credits

Volume 1

CORBIS: 8, 33, 45, 47 (digital image © 1996 CORBIS; original image courtesy of NASA), 48

CORBIS: Aero Graphics, Inc., 7; Tony Arruza, 68; Dave Bartruff, 40; Neil Beer, 61; Patrick Bennett, 27; Bettmann, 95; Bryn Colton/Assignments Photography, 92; Richard Cummins, 87; Sandy Felsenthal, 58; Owen Franken, 1; Marc Garanger, 30; Raymond Gehman, 72; George Hall, 15, 16; Minnesota Historical Society, 93; The National Archives, 71; Richard Olivier, 63, 64; Tim Page, 24; Charles E. Rotkin, 53; Phil Schermeister, 39; Leif Skoogfors, 36; Richard Hamilton Smith, 88, 90; Vince Streano, 82; Geoffrey Taunton/Cordaiy Photo Library, Ltd., 22; Michael S. Yamashita, 85

Volume 2

CORBIS: 51

CORBIS: Annie Griffiths Belt, 76; Bettmann, 46, 64, 68, 74, 86, 90, 104; Jack Fields, 29, 43; Owen Franken, 78; Lowell Georgia, 32; Philip Gould, 93; George Hall, 35, 63; Hulton–Deutsch Collection, 9; Robert Landau, 84; Charles & Josette Lenars, 98; James Marshall, 60; Museum of the City of New York, 53; Gianni Dagli Orti, 49; The Purcell Team, 21; Joel W. Rogers, 54, 56; Hans Georg Roth, 65; Bob Rowan/Progressive Image, 18; Phil Schermeister, 80; Paul A. Souders, 27, 38, 40; Vince Streano, 2, 5; Keren Su, 23; Jim Sugar Photography, 30, 87, 101; Julia Waterlow/Eye Ubiquitous, 73; Nik Wheeler, 83

Volume 3

CORBIS: 37, 46, 99

CORBIS: Bettmann, 3, 19, 24, 26, 29, 52, 75, 83, 86, 102; William Boyce, 59; Stuart Calder/Milepost 92 ½, 78; Ralph A. Clevenger, 80; Leonard de Selva, 84;

Kevin Fleming, 11, 66; Owen Franken, 50; George Hall, 69; Historical Picture Archive, 81, 89; Robert Holmes, 104; Dave G. Houser, 32, 40; Hulton–Deutsch Collection, 6; Bob Krist, 101; George Lepp, 93; Museum of the City of New York, 57; The Purcell Team, 27; Roger Ressmeyer, 16, 25, 43; Galen Rowell, 49, 60; Joseph Sohm/ChromoSohm Inc., 23; Paul A. Souders, 96; Jim Sugar Photography, 9

Volume 4

CORBIS: 6, 10

CORBIS: Bettmann, 46; Jonathan Blair, 3, 52; William A. Blake, 83; Dean Conger, 89; Richard A. Cooke, 96; Randy Faris, 73; Sandy Felsenthal, 30; Ales Fevzer, 47; Owen Franken, 32; Michael Freeman, 12; Colin Garratt/Milepost 92 ½, 76; Robert Garvey, 19; Lowell Georgia, 21; Farrell Grehan, 53, 90; Peter Harholdt, 105; Hulton–Deutsch Collection, 50, 59, 62; Martin Jones/Ecoscene, 15; Wolfgang Kaehl, 70; Catherine Karnow, 4, 69; Kit Kittle, 66; Melvyn P. Lawes/Papilio, 87; Stephanie Maze, 38; Minnesota Historical Society, 60; Richard T. Nowitz, 43; Neil Rabinowitz, 41; Peter Rusell/The Military Picture Library, 25; Leif Skoogfors, 11; Joseph Sohm/ChromoSohm, Inc., 28; Jim Sugar Photography, 35; Patrick Ward, 97; Tim Wright, 33, 55; Yogi, Inc., 14

Volume 5

CORBIS: 9, 62, 66, 70, 78, 89

CORBIS: Bruce Adams/Eye Ubiquitous, 29; AFP, 74; James L. Amos, 48; David Bartruff, 101; Morton Beebe, S.F., 23; Bettman, 39, 92, 94; Jonathan Blair, 6; Gary Braasch, 30; Jan Butchofsky, 1; Dean Conger, 59; Richard Cummins, 38, 86; Lowell Georgia, 33; Dave G. Houser, 4; James Marshall, 43; NASA/Roger Ressmeyer, 80; Roger Ressmeyer, 53, 68, 76; David Samuel Robbins, 87; Bob Rowan/Progressive Image, 13; Galen Rowell, 45, 85; Michael T. Sedam, 105; Richard Hamilton Smith, 84; Paul A. Souders, 21; Jim Sugar Photography, 5; Tim Thompson, 18, 35; Patrick Ward, 16; Karl Weatherly, 12; Yogi, Inc., 98;

Volume 6

CORBIS: 20, 41 (digital image © 1996 CORBIS; original image courtesy of NASA), 52, 66